Martin Luther had a Wife

Harriet Beecher Stowe had a husband

Two books in one special volume

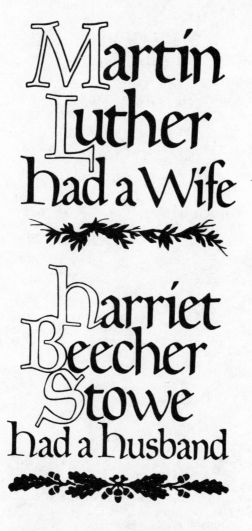

Martin Luther had a Wife

harriet Beecher Stowe had a husband

WILLIAM J. PETERSEN

Tyndale House Publishers, Inc.
Wheaton, Illinois

First printing, February 1983   Tyndale House Pub., Inc.
Library of Congress Catalog Card Number 82-62071
ISBN 0-8423-4104-8, paper
Copyright © 1983 William J. Petersen

HARRIET BEECHER STOWE HAD A HUSBAND
First printing, May 1983   Tyndale House Pubs., Inc.
Library of Congress Catalog Card Number 82-74280
ISBN 0-8423-1329-X
Copyright © 1983 by William J. Petersen

First Combined edition for Christian Herald Family Bookshelf: 1983

Martin Luther had a Wife

WILLIAM J. PETERSEN

First printing, February 1983
Library of Congress Catalog Card Number 82-62071
ISBN 0-8423-4104-8, paper
Copyright © 1983 by William J. Petersen
All rights reserved
Printed in the United States of America

CONTENTS

Of course,
the Christian should
love his wife.
He is supposed
to love his neighbor,
and since his wife
is his nearest neighbor,
she should be
his deepest love.
And she should also
be his dearest friend.

MARTIN
LUTHER

INTRODUCTION

MARRIAGES:
Ordinary, Typical, and Others

"Can This Marriage Be Saved?" *Ladies Home Journal* has sold millions of copies on the basis of that long-running magazine series.

Why is it so successful? Because in it you find that other people are encountering the same marital problems (or shall I call them challenges) that you are facing. And often it is easier to get insight into your own problems when you see them in the lives of others.

A look at the marriages of great Christians should provide you with the same kind of insight. At times, as you read these stories you will be asking the same question: "Can this marriage be saved?"

I call these marriages ordinary marriages. By that, I don't mean that they were bad marriages (some were; some weren't) or humdrum marriages (most weren't). I simply mean that they encountered many of the same problems that couples in your church and in your neighborhood are facing.

Nor do I mean that these were typical marriages. Frankly, I'm not sure what a typical marriage is, anyway. I know that some Christian books and magazine articles talk about ideal and idyllic Christian marriages. But as you read about the marriages described in this book, I don't think you'll want to pray, "Lord, I want a carbon copy of that one," because it conforms perfectly to some imaginary ideal.

The reason for that, I suppose, is that there are no typical people. And when you put two atypical people together in a marriage, you don't come up with a typical marriage, whatever that is.

So, to repeat, I think that you will find these to be ordinary marriages, but not typical marriages.

Of course, greatness, like genius, places unusual stress on a marriage. For one thing, leaders are in the spotlight, and nothing grows normally under such conditions. For another thing, the very gifts and character traits that make a person stand out as a leader may make him or her a challenge as a marriage partner. (Notice that this time I didn't say "problem".)

In the case of the evangelists — Wesley and Moody, for example — travel complicated the marriage. How does a wife cope when a husband is away from home so much of the time? You'll discover that John and Molly Wesley were unable to work out a good solution to the problem.

In the case of the unusually gifted wives — consider Catherine Booth for example — you find conventional roles twisted. How did William Booth handle it?

How did Katie Luther manage to live with her bombastic, blustery husband? And how did Sarah Edwards treat a moody, preoccupied genius?

The problems may loom larger because of the magnitude of the characters, but they are the same kinds of problems that you and your friends and neighbors have to handle in a day of working wives, corporate mobility, business travel, and so on.

In this book you will not find extended treatment of the spiritual accomplishments of these men and women. There are many excellent biographies available, and I hope you will be encouraged to read some of them to learn more of how God worked so mightily through these choice servants of His.

But I was more interested in the ingredients of their marriages. So the emphasis here is on their family backgrounds, the courtship, the marriage's early years (always a crucial time of adjustment), the family relationships, and the two personalities involved.

Of course, there are other fascinating marriages in church history — John Calvin, William Carey,

Adoniram Judson, Harriet Beecher Stowe, and Billy Graham, to name but a few, but these five will serve as a sampler to show you that even the greatest Christians of church history have had rather ordinary marriages and have faced the same kinds of problems that each of us face day by day.

It is my prayer that you will learn as many lessons from them as I have.

CHAPTER ONE

Meet
Martin
and
Katie
Luther

YOU know about Martin Luther, who sparked the Protestant Reformation by nailing his Ninety-Five Theses to the church door in Wittenberg, Germany. But do you know about his wife, Katie, the runaway nun?

She had a quick tongue and he had a quick temper, a combination that does not usually make for a good marriage.

So what kind of a marriage did Martin and Katie have?

A very *unusual* one.

You'll enjoy Katie's outspokenness as well as Martin's colorful outbursts. Martin and Katie seem so human and so contemporary — almost like next-door neighbors. At first you might wonder how their marriage survived. But the better you get to know them, the better you will understand their secret.

"In domestic affairs I defer to Katie. Otherwise I am led by the Holy Ghost." So said Martin Luther, a bit facetiously, about his wife.

"There's a lot to get used to in the first year of marriage," Luther once admitted. "One wakes up in the morning and finds a pair of pigtails on the pillow which were not there before." For the forty-one-year-old former monk and the twenty-six-year-old former nun, there was a lot more than that to get used to.

"I would not change Katie for France or for Venice," Luther said. Once, however, after Katie had contradicted him in front of dinner guests, he sighed and remarked, "If I should ever marry again, I should hew myself an obedient wife out of stone."

Katie was many things for Martin — a gardener, a cook, a nurse, a cattle-raiser, a bookkeeper, and a brewer. But you could never accuse Katie of being a stone. One biographer calls Katie a "quick-witted Saxon with a ready tongue," which made an interesting match for Luther, an intense debater with a short fuse. She could not be described as beautiful with "her longish head, high forehead, long nose, and powerful chin." It was her intelligence and personality that made her attractive to others.

According to one historian, "She ruled both her household and her husband, a situation which the latter accepted resignedly, since he was totally incapable of organizing the affairs of even the smallest household. She brought order into his life and not always to his satisfaction." Martin would probably change that assessment by saying, "She managed the areas that I delegated to her."

There was nothing romantic about the early days of their marriage; Martin Luther was motivated more by duty than by love in pursuing it, and Katie was marrying on the rebound. Yet undeniably a deep love grew between them. Surprisingly, the marriage of Martin and Katie Luther became a model for Protestant marriage.

Who would have thought a few years earlier that either Martin or Katie would get married? And if, by chance, either one got married, who would have thought that either one would have a happy marriage?

Born November 10, 1483, to a copper miner and his wife in Eisleben on the edge of Germany's Thuringian forest, Martin was raised with the strictness that was characteristic of the day in both home and school. Of his parents' strictness, he later rationalized, "They meant well." Regarding the discipline measures used by his early schoolteachers, he asked, "Whoever loved a schoolmaster anyway?" Later, with his own children, he always made sure that there was an apple alongside the rod.

Throughout life he struggled against overbearing and unreasonable authority. At the same time he wanted to be loved. Sometimes shy, he delighted to be in the spotlight; sometimes crude and earthy, he was also warm and devotionally tender. From his father, he picked up a refreshing sense of humor; from his mother, a love of music. He was often moody, sometimes depressed. An indefatigable worker, he often neglected his own health.

No, Martin Luther was not a simple man.

The first major turning point in his life came when he was twenty-one. He had just received his master's degree from the University of Erfurt, and was on his way to a career in law, as his father had wanted.

He was pleasing his father, but there was a Higher Authority that he seemed incapable of pleasing. He felt the wrath of God dangling precariously over his head. "How can you become pious enough to please a holy God?" he asked himself.

One night as he was returning to law school from his parents' home, he was caught in a violent thunderstorm. A bolt of lightning rent the sky, and the twenty-one-year-old law student begged God to spare him, vowing that he would enter a monastery if He would. And two weeks later, he dismayed his parents and shocked his friends by doing just that.

The vows he took were obedience, poverty, and chastity, which of course ruled out marriage. Withdrawing from the world into the monastery, he devoted himself exclusively to prayer. But he was never satisfied that he had the answer to the question, "How can you become pious enough to please a holy God?"

In a few years he was transferred to a monastery in Wittenberg, and was named lecturer in Bible studies at the new university there. As he began to teach God's Word — particularly the Epistles of Romans and Galatians — he made a new discovery. Righteousness does not come by works; it is imputed to us by faith. It does not come by what we do, but by what Christ has already done in our behalf. He termed it a "wonderful new definition of righteousness." Martin Luther had grasped the meaning of Paul's expression, "The just shall live by faith."

In 1517, when he was thirty-three, Martin Luther nailed his Ninety-Five Theses to the Wittenberg door, seeking a scholarly debate. He never got the debate; he got a Reformation instead.

Four years later, he was called to appear before the Diet of Worms, where Emperor Charles V, Archduke Ferdinand, six Prince Electors, dukes, archbishops, papal nuncios, ambassadors — a total of 200 dignitaries — were gathered. Although he knew his life was at stake, Martin Luther refused to retract what he had written. His authority was not the church nor the Pope; his authority was the Bible itself, the Word of God. "Here I stand. I can do no other. God help me."

A few days later, the Edict of Worms condemned both Luther and his writings and asked all citizens for their help in arresting him. If they preferred, they could kill Luther on sight.

Luther, however, had left Worms before the edict was signed. On the way back to Wittenberg, friends "kidnapped" him and secretly took him to the Castle of Wartburg, where he remained in exile for eight months, translating the Bible into German.

He was thirty-seven years old now, and still considered himself under the vows he had taken when he had entered the monastery sixteen years earlier. Later, he said, "If anyone had told me, when I was at the Diet of Worms: 'In a few years you will have a wife and be sitting at home,' I should not have believed it."

Before Worms, Luther had been a folk hero of all those who were unhappy with the status quo.

While he was in his Wartburg captivity, Luther's reformation started moving in directions that bewildered him: Monks, as well as priests, began to renounce their vows and get married, and this caused Luther to reexamine his own thinking about the vows of celibacy that he had taken.

Luther's first expression was: "Good heavens, they won't give *me* a wife."

Called back to Wittenberg to restore order to the turbulent movement he had spawned, Luther was upset by religious fanatics on one hand and political radicals on the other. Ignorant religionists were led by visions rather than the Word, and in Luther's absence had drawn away some of those that previously had been disciples of the Wittenberg reformer. On the other hand, peasants were rising up against their feudal lords and claiming the backing of Luther's writings.

When Luther disowned their cause, he was no longer their hero. Many even viewed him as a traitor.

In Saxony (east central Germany) Luther was relatively safe because the ruler of Saxony, Frederick the Wise, had promised the reformer protection. But outside of Saxony, he could travel only at his own risk.

Thus in 1525, eight years after he had penned his Ninety-Five Theses in Wittenberg and four years after he had made his courageous "Here I stand" defense at Worms, Luther was hunted by the Pope, hated by the peasants, and harassed by the religious fanatics. At forty-one, he had good reason to feel that the bloom was gone from the Reformation rose.

And that was the year that Martin Luther married. His bride was Katherine von Bora.

Katherine, nearly sixteen years younger than Martin, had been placed in a nunnery when she was only nine or ten years old. Her father had just remarried and Katie's quick wit and sharp tongue did not endear her to her stepmother. So off to the nunnery. Six years later she took her vows.

In the early 1520s, tracts by Martin Luther began appearing mysteriously within the cloistered walls of Katie's nunnery. Furthermore, rumors had been circulating that elsewhere nuns and monks were leaving their monastic houses to follow this man who was teaching that salvation was a gift from God, not to be earned by religious observances.

Secretly Katie and eleven other nuns sent word to Luther in Wittenberg that they were interested in leaving the nunnery. Could he help them? Security, however, was tight and the nunnery was located in territory ruled by Duke George, an archenemy of Luther. Already Duke George had executed one man for devising an escape plan for some nuns. Luther had to come up with a fool-proof plan.

In the nearby town of Torgau was a respected senior citizen named Leonard Kopp. A member of the town council and a former Torgau tax collector, he had the contract to deliver barrels of smoked herring to the cloister in Nimbschen which housed the twelve unhappy nuns. Exactly how Kopp did it is unknown, but somehow when he arrived, his canvas-covered wagon seemed to be carrying twelve barrels of smoked herring, and when he left it seemed to be loaded with twelve empty barrels underneath the canvas. But the barrels were not empty.

Two days later, nine nuns (three had returned to their parents' homes) were delivered to Martin Luther's doorstep, and it was Luther's job to find either positions or husbands for them. Finding jobs for them wouldn't be easy. The nuns weren't trained in housekeeping. One historian commented, "All they could do was pray and sing." To find husbands for them would not be easy either. Since German girls usually married at age fifteen or sixteen, most of the nuns were considerably past their prime. But Martin Luther felt obligated to help them. "I feel so sorry for them; they are a wretched little bunch," he wrote to a friend.

Someone suggested that maybe Luther could help solve his problem by marrying one of them himself. He responded that he wouldn't think of it, not because he was a sexless stone or against marriage, but because he thought he might soon be killed as a heretic. Evidently by this time, he no longer considered himself obligated to continue his monk's vow.

Eventually, Luther was able to find husbands for some of the nuns, but one of them remained as his biggest problem. It was Katie von Bora, who had found temporary employment in the home of Lucas Cranach, Luther's neighbor. Cranach had a large household and he seemed to need all the domestic help he could get.

It wasn't as if no one wanted her. Her personality and quick wit attracted the attention of a young man from a distinguished family in Nuremburg, and the two fell in love. But when he returned to tell his parents that he wished to marry a runaway nun, they refused him permission.

The rejection struck Katie hard, and she was heartbroken. But Luther the matchmaker didn't give up trying. Determined to find a husband for Katie, he soon had someone else in mind. Unfortunately the next candidate didn't suit Katie, though Luther thought that she could ill afford to be fussy. Katie sent word back that while she wasn't at all against the idea of marriage, she would never marry the latest candidate; in fact, to underscore her willingness to marry, she thought she would mention a couple possible candidates herself — even though it was obvious to friends that she was still in love with the young man from Nuremburg. Amsdorf, one of Luther's fellow professors at Wittenberg, was one candidate that she would be willing to marry; the other was Luther himself. Amsdorf, like Luther, was in his early forties.

The message from Katie got back to Luther at a very propitious time. Rumors had been circulating across Europe of the nine nuns who had been camping on Luther's doorstep. Luther's enemies — and they were legion — imagined the worst. There were jokes about Luther's harem. Katie was the only one left, and the rumors were stronger than ever. There was only one nun, but now there were nine times as many rumors.

In April 1525, shortly after he received Katie's message about the two eligible candidates for her hand, Martin visited his aged parents. His father, who had never wanted his son to become a monk, was pleased that Martin had left the monastery. Now only one thing remained before his son could say that he had made a complete break with the past. He would have to marry and father children to carry on the family name.

Luther had been preaching for several years that marriage was a divinely established institution. To elevate celibacy above marriage was unbiblical. Now it was time for him to practice what he had been preaching.

It was a big step for the forty-one-year-old monk to take. With the exception of his parents, he seemed to take counsel with no one else. Even many of his closest friends were unaware of the decision he was struggling with.

Some of his friends had deserted him. His national popularity had waned and his spiritual impact was fragmenting. In some ways, he felt he would have to start all over again. Perhaps at age forty-one he could begin afresh.

What better way than to get married and start a family? As he thought about it, his marriage would "please his father, rile the Pope, make angels laugh and devils weep, and would seal his testimony." Perhaps it would even shut the mouths of the rumormongers.

And hadn't Katie practically proposed to him?

The closest thing to a counter-proposal came when he told Katie that he might be burned at the stake, and if she was wed to him, it might mean her life as well. Apparently, the peril didn't dissuade Katie.

The courtship was anything but romantic. "I am not madly in love, but I cherish her," said Luther.

On June 10, 1525, Luther wrote, "The gifts of God must be taken on the wing." So once he made up his mind, Luther didn't waste any time.

The wedding took place June 13. Lucas Cranach and his wife were witnesses. The suddenness of it caused more rumors to fly and even some close friends like Philipp Melanchthon had second thoughts about it. But as Luther later remarked, "If I had not married quickly and secretly and taken few into my confidence, everyone would have done what he could to hinder me; for all my friends said: 'Not this one, but another.' " Many of them thought that Luther should have married a more distinguished woman than Katie, the runaway nun.

Even Luther had to pinch himself to make sure it wasn't a dream. "I can hardly believe it myself," he joked, "but the witnesses are too strong." And when he invited the herring distributor Leonard Kopp to the wedding, he wrote, "God likes to work miracles and to make a fool of the world. You must come to the wedding."

Their first recorded argument came over a wedding gift — a present of twenty guilders (about two months' salary for Martin) given by Archbishop Albrecht of Mainz. Albrecht was an enemy and Luther wanted nothing to do with his guilders. After all, it was Albrecht who had authorized the selling of indulgences which had prompted Luther's Ninety-Five Theses.

But thrifty Katie, who had picked up some household economics from her experience in the Cranach home, knew that Martin had an indebtedness of one hundred guilders, and she felt that a wedding gift of twenty guilders should be received as from the Lord, no matter through whose hands it may have passed. Luther gave in. The practical outweighed the emotional.

For both of them, the first year of marriage meant great adjustments. Martin had not made his bed in a year. "Before I married, no one had made up my bed for a whole year. The straw was rotting from my sweat. I wore myself out with work during the day, so that I fell into bed oblivious of everything." That was changed now. Katie even gave him a pillow.

For someone who had lived alone as long as Martin had, it wasn't easy to take someone else's views into consideration, but Katie's personality injected itself forcefully into Martin's decision-making processes. For instance, he had planned to go to a friend's wedding. When he told Katie where it was, she put up a fuss. Marauding bands of peasants were known to be in the area and they were angry about some of Luther's writings. Katie thought it would be unwise to travel through their territory. Luther deferred to Katie's judgment.

But Martin's biggest adjustment dealt with the family's purse strings. He had never learned how to handle money. He once said, "God divided the hand into fingers so that money would slip through." He was "loath to accept anything not absolutely necessary, and he would give away anything not absolutely required."

With Katie as his business manager, fiscal planning was introduced. As one biographer puts it, Frau Luther's thrift enabled the Luthers to "accumulate a considerable property, notwithstanding her husband's unbounded liberality and hospitality." At times she had to hide money to keep Martin from giving it away. Martin would invite students to come and live with them, but Katie insisted that they pay room and board.

The Wittenberg bank didn't appreciate Martin's penchant for overdrawing his account, but he explained with a strange lack of logic, "I do not worry about debts anymore, because when Katie pays one, another comes due."

While there were tensions in this area, Martin soon came to understand his deficiencies and Katie's strengths in household management. "The greatest blessing," Luther once wrote, probably thinking of Katie, "is to have a wife to whom you may entrust your affairs."

There is some indication that early in his marriage Martin was concerned enough about their financial situation to do something about it. He installed a lathe, perhaps thinking that he could go into business if his government stipend was cut off. There is no record that he ever used the lathe, however, and his philosophy was always "The Lord will provide."

Martin's best work was done in front of books, not in front of a lathe.

He had to adjust to working with people around him. In the monastery he had been accustomed to being secluded, but Katie wouldn't stand for that. According to one story, he once locked himself in his study for three days until Katie had the door removed. Innocently, Martin asked as he saw Katie standing in the doorless doorway, "Why did you do that? I wasn't doing any harm."

Katie wasn't content to be a Martha, working in the kitchen or garden. But Luther didn't always want to be bothered by a Mary. She liked to sit at Martin's side while he read. "During the first year," Martin told some friends, "my Katie would sit at my side while I was working, and when she was at a loss for something to say, she would ask me: 'Is the Grand Master of Prussia the brother of the Margrave?' "

Even after the children came — and they had six children — Martin, who was adjusting well to doing his work in a fishbowl atmosphere, often wanted to withdraw into himself at the time when Katie wanted to share his world. As biographer Roland Bainton points out, "The rhythm of work and rest did not coincide for Luther and his wife. After a day with children, animals and servants, she wanted to talk with an equal; and he, after preaching four times, lecturing and conversing with students at meals, wanted to drop into a chair and sink into a book." And then Katie might ask him a question about the Grand Master of Prussia or about predestination or why David in the Psalms bragged about his own righteousness when he really didn't have any.

"All my life is patience," said Luther, who must have recognized that patience wasn't his strongest virtue. "I have to be patient with the Pope; I have to be patient with the heretics; I have to be patient with my family; and I even have to be patient with Katie." Katie had to be even more patient with her genius husband. He was a man of many moods; melancholy was often induced by poor health, and sometimes vice versa. "I think that my illnesses are not natural, but are mere bewitchments," he once said. Another time, he said, "I am so ill, but no one believes me." He had a shopping list of ailments including gout, insomnia, catarrh, hemorrhoids, constipation, stone (gallstones or kidney stones), dizziness, and ringing in the ears.

Katie patiently nursed him back to health with proper diet, herbs, poultices, and massages. But once after she gave him some medicine for his migraine headaches, he responded: "My best prescription is written in the third chapter of John: 'For God so loved the world, that he gave his only begotten Son, that whosoever believeth in him should not perish, but have eternal life.' "

Katie was far more than chief cook, nurse, and bottle-washer. She had to be a remarkable woman to manage the ever-expanding Luther household. The Augustinian monastery where Luther had lived as a monk was deeded to Martin and Katie jointly by the government. On the first floor it had forty rooms with cells above for sleeping; at times every room was occupied. Besides the six Luther children, a half dozen of Martin's nieces and nephews were brought in, out of the goodness of his heart. Then when a friend lost his wife in a plague, Luther brought home the four children. To cope with the growing household, Katie in turn brought in some of her relatives, including Aunt Magdalena, who became a "nanny" for the Luther children and was nicknamed Mummie Lena.

Besides the children, there were tutors and student boarders, and of course due to Luther's fame, guests dropped in unexpectedly from England, Hungary, and elsewhere. One prince had been planning to take a room at the monastery for a few days, but changed his mind. He had received a letter, telling him the nature of the place: "An odd assortment of young people, students, young widows, old women and children lives in the Doctor's home; this makes for great disquiet."

But more and more the gregarious Luther thrived in the bustling atmosphere. The students who got the benefit of Luther's formal lectures during the day plied him with questions during the supper hour and the reformer's famed *Table Talks* emerged. Katie would be at the far end of the table surrounded by the children while the students were taking notes close to her husband. No doubt, she was a bit jealous that they were able to get closer to Dr. Luther than she could at the supper hour, but she knew her husband needed the attention. When she found out that the students were taking notes which they intended to publish, however, she wanted to charge them for note-taking privileges. Martin wouldn't let her do it. Later these students published 6596 entries in their various versions of *Table Talks*. If Katie had had her way, she would have had a guilder for each entry.

At times, during these informal supper sessions, Luther's language became coarse or crude and Katie would have to rebuff him: "Oh, come now, that's too raw."

That happened often enough, for Luther was not known for delicacy of speech. But more often than that, he would spend the entire supper hour talking. When Katie, who didn't mince words, would say, "Doctor, why don't you stop talking and eat?" he would respond with something like: "Women should repeat the Lord's Prayer before opening their mouths."

Katie called him "Doctor" in public conversation. Martin called her anything that came into his mind. Sometimes thinking of Eve, he called her "my rib." More often, thinking of the way she managed the manor, he called her "my lord." Sometimes, he called her "my chain," a pun on the German *Kethe*.

During the day, children played in Martin Luther's study. Once he told of his son Hans: "As I sit and write, he sings me a song, and if it gets too loud I scold him a little, but he goes on singing just the same."

Luther says he learned much from his children, although he was amused by their silly play: "Christ said we must become as little children to enter the kingdom of heaven. Dear God, this is too much. Have we got to become such idiots?"

Besides being a good mother and efficient housekeeper, Katie proved to be a wise manager of the farms, gardens, cattle, and livestock that the Luther family came to own, thanks to her prudent and expansive policies. She also took care of the small family brewery, and Luther frequently praised his wife's ability to make good beer.

Katie remodelled the monastery, installing a bathroom and putting in three cellars with an extra stairway. Because she had a goal to make their large household self-supporting, she grew peas, beans, turnips, melons, and lettuce in their vegetable garden and eight different fruits in their orchard. (One year, her husband magnanimously took care of the garden.) Begrudgingly, Martin gave his consent to her to buy a second garden. The deciding factor was that a brook ran through it. Katie was able to hook quite a few fish from the brook for their supper table. Their livestock included eight pigs, five cows, nine calves, as well as chickens, pigeons, geese, and a dog named Tolpel that Luther hoped to meet in heaven. All of these were Katie's responsibility, and she even played the role of veterinary surgeon to do the job properly.

Martin wasn't exactly happy about the fact that Katie inherited a farm in Zulsdorf, a two-day journey from Wittenberg. He didn't appreciate the amount of time that Katie spent there; for Katie it was a retreat from the hubbub of the Wittenberg monastery.

One letter Martin wrote her was addressed: "To the rich lady of Zulsdorf, who lives in the flesh at Wittenberg, but in the spirit at Zulsdorf."

Her land was her empire, and like an emperor she always had her mind set on conquering new worlds and annexing them to her kingdom. One farm she looked at was only an hour away from Wittenberg. Martin stalled her long enough to give someone else the time to buy it. Once Martin wrote her, "Oh, Katie, you have a husband who loves you. Let someone else be an empress."

In a letter to a friend, Martin once wrote: "My lord Katie greets you. She plants our fields, pastures and sells cows et cetera. In between she has started to read the Bible. I have promised her fifty guilders if she finishes by Easter. She is hard at it and is at the end of the fifth book of Moses."

It's a wonder that she had time to read the book of Jude, much less the entire Bible. But Luther kept on prodding her to keep at her Bible reading, until she responded, "Would to God I lived up to it!"

When Katie became frustrated with a project, she was apt to strike her side and burst forth with an "Ave Maria," to which Luther would respond, "Why don't you ask Christ to help you?"

They teased each other in good humor. Once while he was traveling, Luther wrote home: "To the saintly, worrying Lady Katherine Luther, doctor at Zulsdorf [the home of her inherited farm] and Wittenberg, my gracious, dear wife. We thank you heartily for being so worried that you can't sleep, for since you started worrying about us, a fire broke out near my door, and yesterday, no doubt due to your worry, a big stone, save for the dear angels, would have fallen and crushed us like a mouse in a trap. If you don't stop worrying, I'm afraid the earth will swallow us. Pray and let God worry. Cast your burden on the Lord."

Martin's appreciation of marriage deepened during his twenty years with Katie. Marriage is a school for character, and both he and Katie learned much in that school. They learned from each other, from their children, and from their mutual experiences. The father, said Luther one day, even learns from his experience of hanging out the diapers to the amusement of his neighbors. "Let them laugh," he concluded. "God and the angels smile in heaven."

He thought of the miracle at Cana in John 2 as a parable of marriage. "The first love," he once said, "is drunken. When the intoxication wears off, then comes the real married love." The best wine is saved for last. There may be times when it may appear that the wine is running out. "I will not take the vexation out of marriage. I may even increase it, but it will turn out wonderfully, as they only know who have tasted it."

Since both Martin and Katie had quick tongues, arguments were not foreign to the Luther household. "But," said Martin, "think of all the squabbles Adam and Eve must have had in the course of their 900 years. Eve would say, 'You ate the apple' and Adam would retort, 'You gave it to me.' "

With all the bantering, the Luthers had a good marriage. "To have peace and love in marriage is a gift which is next to the knowledge of the Gospel," he once said. And no one could deny that the Luthers had that gift.

Before his marriage, Luther sometimes spoke of matrimony as a necessity for the flesh. Afterwards, he emphasized it was an opportunity for the spirit. He came to decry the fact that many men were marrying only for physical reasons, were abusing their wives, and knew nothing about love. Marriage is no joke, he said; it must be worked on, and prayed over.... "To get a wife is easy enough, but to love her with constancy is difficult...for the mere union of the flesh is not sufficient; there must be a congeniality of tastes and character. And that congeniality does not come overnight.

"Some marriages were motivated by mere lust," Luther once said, "but mere lust is felt even by fleas and lice. Love begins when we wish to serve others.

"Of course, the Christian should love his wife," Luther declared. "He is supposed to love his neighbor, and since his wife is his nearest neighbor, she should be his deepest love. And she should also be his dearest friend."

That this friendship existed between Martin and Katie is obvious from the frequency of Luther's references to his wife. When he spoke of Paul's Epistle to the Galatians, the reading of which led to his spiritual rebirth, he called it "my Katharina von Bora." It was the epistle that was the closest to his heart.

Once when he was stressing the importance of trusting Christ in daily matters, he confessed: "I trust more in Katie and I expect more from Katie than I do Christ." Perhaps it testified more to his relationship with his wife than it did to a lack of commitment to Jesus Christ.

"Nothing is more sweet than harmony in marriage, and nothing more distressing than dissension," Luther said and no doubt his marriage had moments of both. "Next to it is the loss of a child. I know how that hurts."

The Luthers lost their second child before she was a year old and their third, Magdalena, in her fourteenth year. "How strange it is that she is at peace and I am so sorrowful," he said at her death.

But children brought much joy to the home. Referring to his children, he said, "God has given to me greater gifts than to any bishop in a thousand years." Yet the children were certainly normal, active youngsters. To one of them, Luther cried out, "Child, what have you done that I should love you so? What with your befouling the corners and bawling through the whole house." In 1531, watching Katie fondle their youngest son, Martin, he remarked, "Surely God must talk with me even more fondly than my Katie with her little Martin."

When Luther was fifty-nine, their daughter Magdalena died. It was a severe blow to Luther at a time when he was beset with other trials as well. His health was worsening and he was involved in several major religious disputes.

Outside the home, he was becoming increasingly bitter, cantankerous, and unbending. Some of his friends felt that he might undo all that he had accomplished in his earlier years. But the home was a refuge for him and there is no indication that Luther's external problems soured its atmosphere.

On his deathbed, Luther admonished: "If it be God's will, accept it." Katie responded: "My dear doctor, if it is God's will, I would rather have you with our Lord than here. Don't worry about us. God will take care of us."

In 1546 at the age of sixty-two, Martin died. Katie died four years later. Her last words were "I will stick to Christ as a burr to a topcoat."

Martin may have been the key figure in the Protestant Reformation, but Martin and Katie together revolutionized the common concept of marriage that was held in that day.

There was a saying that Martin loved to quote: "Let the wife make her husband glad to come home and let him make her sorry to see him leave."

The success of any marriage depends on two people who aren't afraid to grow and change as Martin and Katie did.

CHAPTER
TWO

Meet
John
and
Molly
Wesley

MOST of you don't need to be introduced to John Wesley, the father of the worldwide Methodist movement. You sing the hymns written by John and his brother Charles. You are aware of his Aldersgate experience, and the entire world has been affected by John's concerns for evangelism and personal holiness.

But you have probably never encountered Molly Goldhawk Vazeille Wesley, John's wife.

Maybe, after I've introduced you, you will wish you had never met her.

I can guarantee, however, as you interact with John and Molly, that you will have much cause for thought.

What were the factors that made it such a miserable marriage?

How could it have been otherwise?

What can you learn from it to avoid in your own marriage?

One of the early Wesley biographers stated that, along with Xanthippe and Job's wife, Mrs. John Wesley had to be rated as one of the worst wives in all history.

A later biographer responded by saying that if that was so, then surely John Wesley must be regarded as one of the worst husbands in history.

Both allegations seem quite extreme.

But what are you to do with the story that Molly Wesley was seen dragging her husband around the room by his hair?

And what about the correspondence that John Wesley continued to maintain, despite his wife's objections, with his female admirers?

John Wesley is well known as the intrepid evangelist of Methodism who traveled a quarter of a million miles on horseback, who claimed the world as his parish, and who rose at four each morning for his devotional time. But his home was a shambles. Four years after his marriage, he wrote to his brother Charles, "Love is rot."

He preached 42,000 sermons, often preaching four or five times a day during his fifty-three-year ministry. Crowds of up to 30,000 came to hear him preach. When he died at the age of eighty-eight, Methodism had 153,000 adherents, and the movement had spread to America as well as to Holland, Ireland, and Scotland.

He was a remarkable man and God used him mightily. Yet his marriage was a miserable failure.

He waited for marriage until he was forty-seven; he probably waited too long. (Some would say he didn't wait long enough.) He had serious romances when he was twenty-five, thirty-five, and forty-five. He retreated from each one at the last minute. Perhaps any one of the three would have provided him a happier marriage than he had with Molly. But had Wesley had a happier marriage, we might not have had the outgrowth of the formidable Methodist movement.

In order to understand John Wesley and his problems in marriage, you have to take a glimpse of the fascinating home in which he was reared.

John Wesley was the fifteenth of nineteen children born to Samuel and Susanna Wesley. Samuel was a stern, argumentative Anglican cleric who spent most of his ministry in an out-of-the-way parish, trying to exhort a bunch of uneducated ruffians. His biggest joy in life seemed to be when he could get away from Epworth to go to Convocation in London. It had been an honor for him to be named to this top-ranking study commission; it was a joy as well because during the sessions he got to argue theology with eminent theologians.

At home, he argued with his wife, Susanna, a well-educated, well-bred woman who wanted the best for her husband and for her children, and who had a reason for everything she did.

Both Susanna and Samuel were stubborn, and Samuel had a quick temper besides. Once during family prayers, after Samuel had properly prayed for the reigning English monarch, King William of Orange, he noted that his wife had not said her traditional "amen." In fact, come to think of it, she had not said the appropriate "amen" for several days. The reason was obvious. Susanna did not favor King William of Orange; she thought he was a usurper of the throne. She favored the Stuart line. So, in Susanna's words, her husband "immediately kneeled down and imprecated the divine vengeance upon himself and all his posterity if ever he touched me more or came into bed with me before I had begged God's pardon and his."

Whereupon Samuel left for a timely Convocation in London. King William soon died, which was an answer to prayer for Susanna and maybe even for the equally stubborn Samuel, because upon William's death Queen Anne, a Stuart, came to the throne. Thereafter Susanna could say "amen" when her husband prayed for the reigning monarch.

The story is typical of the marriage. Here are some quotes from Susanna's writings: "Since I'm willing to let him quietly enjoy his opinions, he ought not to deprive me of my little liberty of conscience." And "I think we are not likely to live happily together." And another, "It is a misfortune peculiar to our family that he and I seldom think alike."

A little more than nine months after the coronation of Queen Anne, John Wesley, the fifteenth of the Wesleys' nineteen children, was born. Nine of the children died at birth or in infancy, and that left ten to be raised on the modest income derived from the remote parish of Epworth. When John — or "Jackie" as his mother called him — was only two years old, his father was imprisoned for three months for his inability tc pay a thirty-pound debt. During his prison term, his biggest concern was his family, but he wrote, "My wife bears it with the courage which becomes her and which I expected from her."

Later when Samuel was in London attending another of the lengthy Convocations, an interim minister preached in his pulpit and made repeated aspersions about the regular minister's chronic indebtedness and about other foibles that Samuel undeniably had.

When the congregation dwindled, Susanna began holding evening services in her kitchen. Soon her evening flock outnumbered those in the morning congregation at the Epworth church. The interim rector didn't like it. He wrote to Samuel in London urging him to take immediate action and stop this outrage. Simultaneously, Susanna wrote, justifying her actions. Something needed to be done, she said, and no man in the congregation had as strong a voice as she had; furthermore no one else could read well enough to lead the congregation in the prayerbook and the reading of the sermon. She said that although she knew that God approved of what she was doing, she would submit to her husband if he would definitely put his foot down. But he had to say so definitely. Then she asked her husband if he wanted to put his foot down or not. The way she wrote it was like this: "Do not tell me that you desire me not to do it, for that will not satisfy my conscience; but send me your positive command in such full and express terms as may absolve me from all guilt and punishment for neglecting this opportunity of doing good, when you and I shall appear before the great and awful tribunal of our Lord Jesus Christ."

Samuel Wesley decided that since the problem would go away as soon as he returned home in a few weeks, he would take no immediate action.

As if the Wesleys didn't have enough troubles, the old parsonage caught fire one night in 1709. Nearly everything was lost, but fortunately the children had all escaped to the garden. All except one. Five-year-old John was missing. The father tried to reenter the house but the smoke and flames made the stairway impassable. Finally a ladder was brought and was raised to little John's window. The boy was saved, just before the roof collapsed.

Susanna called it divine intervention and spoke of John as "a brand plucked from the burning." After the dramatic rescue, while she was mindful of the spiritual welfare of all her children, she was especially concerned about young John. She had made a resolution to be "particularly careful of the soul of this child, which God had so mercifully provided for."

Susanna raised her children strictly. At the age of one year, they were instructed to cry softly when they had to cry. She took responsibility for their early education, and her daughters were treated as the educational equals of her sons. She regimented her spiritual activities and expected her children to do accordingly. She assigned a day of the week when she would take time to provide personalized scriptural and moral instruction to her children. Each child was assigned a day; John's day was Thursday.

Growing up, John was tended by seven sisters. Later most of the sisters, like John himself, experienced unhappy marriages. Where the blame lies for the string of mismatches is hard to tell. Some blame the father who had a knack for crushing his daughters' promising love affairs, until in rebellion they ran off with totally unsuitable mates. One of the daughters openly spoke of the father's "unaccountable love of discord." His paternal concern made him censorious and overly protective.

Samuel Wesley was a man who had never come to terms with himself. His parish was too small and remote. He wasn't properly appreciated in the community. At home he was frustrated by his inability to cope with Susanna and his children. And at times this frustration erupted irrationally.

Susanna herself was such a dominant force that her influence was indelibly imprinted on her children's personalities — especially on John's. She was John's spiritual advisor until her death when John was thirty-nine. For years they read and discussed the same books. One biographer says: "Hers was the decisive voice that sent her two sons on their ill-starred mission to Georgia; it was to her steadfastness that John looked for reassurance when he returned to England with his faith shaken and his future in jeopardy. As soon as he had a settled home, his mother became its permanent inmate. He himself admitted that in his early youth he put aside all thoughts of marriage through despair of finding any woman her equal."

John Wesley grew up with his mother's logical mind. His brother Charles was heir to their father's poetic flair. But John became a skilled debater with a love for wit and humor. His wit and humor made him quite popular during his youth. One of his sisters said that no one could be sad when John was around.

At seventeen, John went to Oxford University where he studied the classics and had his first serious romance. One of the earliest entries in his diary, which he kept for more than sixty years, asks, "Have I loved a woman or company more than God?" It was a question that plagued him through the years.

There were four young women in a circle of friends, and John had an interest in each of them. He wrote to his mother about Betty Kirkham, describing her as a "religious friend," but it is obvious from his diary that she was a special kind of religious friend. However, after waiting several years for John's expressions of affection to materialize in a proposal of marriage, Betty Kirkham accepted the hand of another suitor. His diary indicates that he had thought of marriage, but something had kept him from it.

He kept his friendship with Betty alive for several years — even though her husband was jealous of Wesley's attention to his wife. John at the same time was beginning his solicitations of another young woman in the circle. When the only way the relationship could progress any further was by a proposal of marriage, John backed away again.

Mabel Brailsford in her *Tale of Two Brothers* writes: "The pattern had now been set for all John's abortive love affairs: the bright beginning, the hesitation and long shilly-shallying: the exasperation of the lady and her ultimatum, quickly rescinded but not quickly enough to forestall his final renunciation. Three times he would be upon the brink of marriage and three times he would extricate himself before the decisive word had been spoken. Each time his affections were more deeply involved."

John was twenty-nine now, had his master's degree from Oxford, had been appointed a teaching fellow and had, with his brother Charles, started the "Holy Club," a group that because of its methodical way of attaining spirituality became known as the Methodists.

His seventy-year-old father wanted him to take over his parish at Epworth, but John refused the offer, wanting to stay at Oxford, where he could promote his own holiness. He told his father that only where he himself could be holy could he effectively promote the holiness of others.

At this point in his life, John preferred the role of tutor to that of professor. He wanted to disciple those who were earnestly seeking the path of salvation. But he had two problems: (1) he was not sure of his own salvation and (2) he was very naive about those who pretended to be spiritually minded, especially young spiritually minded women. To be blunt, John was much more attractive to women than he realized.

This was clearly seen in 1735 when he was appointed as a chaplain to accompany James Oglethorpe to the new colony of Georgia in America. John's job in America would be to assist the motley band of settlers — ex-convicts, Jews, German exiles, and debtors — and to preach to the heathen Indians whom he considered to be "little children, humble, willing to learn." But Wesley's main reason for going to America was simply in his own words: "My chief motive, to which all the rest are subordinate, is the hope of saving my own soul." He was also quite certain that in Georgia he would no longer be tempted by the lusts of the flesh for he would "no longer see any woman, but those which are almost of a different species from me."

He didn't realize how wrong he was.

On board ship, John was "in jeopardy every hour," as he wrote in his diary. He thought of asking his brother Charles to pray for him, because of the many young women aboard, some of whom were feigning spiritual interest. He felt he needed prayer that he should "know none of them after the flesh."

When a storm arose on the Atlantic, he realized he was in jeopardy another way. The German Moravians on board seemed to be the only passengers who were calm in the face of what seemed to John to be a possible grave in the angry deep. When John asked the reason for their serenity, he in return was asked a few questions: "Do you know Jesus Christ?" "Do you know you are a child of God?" "Do you know you are saved?"

John was perplexed. He was a minister and a son of a minister. He was even a missionary and he was rigorously practicing holiness, elusive though it was, and he was intent on pursuing it even if his chase took him around the world. But he had to admit that he did not possess the calm assurance of salvation that the Moravians had.

After arriving on *terra firma* in America, things did not improve. Though he attended to his disciplines faithfully — arising at four, services at five, etc. — he was ineffective both as a minister to the settlers and as a missionary to the Indians.

But he was not ineffective in reaching the heart of Sophy Hopkey, the eighteen-year-old niece of Savannah's chief magistrate. John, now thirty-three, found in Sophy everything he wanted in a woman. She was "all stillness and attention" when he read books of sermons to her. She was quick to learn when he instructed her in French grammar. She was also quite ready for marriage, since she was unhappy at home with her aunt and uncle.

John didn't know what to do. When he was with her, he confessed that he was under the weight of "an unholy desire." He admitted to her that he would like to spend the rest of his life with her. Half the colony, it seemed, was urging him to marry the girl, but John pulled away from the flame. "I find, Miss Sophy, I cannot take fire into my bosom and not be burnt. I am therefore retiring for awhile to desire the direction of God."

Getting away from Sophy didn't solve the problem. So for his definitive answer on whether to get married or not, he decided to draw lots. One slip of paper said, "Marry"; another, "Not this year"; a third, "Think of it no more." The third slip of paper was drawn.

Though John still found it difficult, he broke up with Sophy. By the end of the year, John had returned to England. In his journal, he described his break with Sophy as an escape, and that once again he was "a brand snatched from the burning." On his way back to England, he had several weeks to think about his missionary term in America. It had lasted less than two years, and John was realistic enough to assess it as a failure.

But six months later, Wesley's new life began. Depressed, he attended a meeting near Aldersgate Street in London and listened to the reading of Luther's *Commentary on Romans*. Wesley felt his heart "strangely warmed." He had been converted. He had discovered "salvation by faith only." Now he knew Jesus as the German Moravians did.

A year later, in 1739, Wesley began his preaching in the fields. The crowds were huge. Wesley estimated twenty thousand at some of the preaching services. Quickly the work expanded. A school for poor children was started at Kingswood; a new meeting house was built in Bristol. An old cannon foundry near Moorfields was transformed into a 1500-seat chapel.

During the next fifty years, he crisscrossed England on horseback over rough country roads, preaching the gospel nine months a year, starting

Methodist societies all across the British Isles. Wesley became one of the dominant figures of the eighteenth century.

It was during the early years of this itinerant ministry that he met Grace Murray and entered into his most serious love affair. Grace Murray was in her late twenties, the widow of a sailor. Converted by Wesley's preaching, she soon became the leading woman Methodist, addressing the women's classes.

In 1748, Wesley, now forty-five, became ill and was tended by the "amiable, pious and efficient" Mrs. Murray. John didn't exactly propose to her on the spot, but he did say, "If ever I marry, I think you will be the person." The widow Murray was flattered by his attention.

When Wesley was well enough to resume his preaching schedule, Grace was asked to join the troupe. A few months later John conducted evangelistic missions in Ireland and Grace was once again a part of his team. In fact, she rode on the same horse behind Wesley. Wesley reported on her ministry, "She examined all the women in the smaller societies, and the believers in every place. She settled all the women bands, visited the sick, prayed with the mourners." She was, as one report has stated, the only coworker with whom John was able to work closely for a long period of time.

John was deeply in love with Grace and he debated the pros and cons of matrimony. As usual, he kept a scorecard. In all seven marriage areas (housekeeper, nurse, companion, friend, fellow-laborer in the gospel of Christ, spiritual gifts, and spiritual fruit from her labors), he rated Grace as excellent. He concluded, "Therefore all my seven arguments against marriage are totally set aside. Nay some of them seem to prove, both that I ought to marry and that G. M. is the Person." G. M. was his business-efficient way of referring to Grace Murray.

John realized that there might be some problems. For instance, what about children? His solution would be to place the children in the Methodist school at Kingswood while he and his wife continued their evangelistic ministry. One writer commented: "He was incapable of real domesticity; he wanted a coadjutor, not a wife."

But John faced some other obstacles too, the biggest of which was his own procrastination. And then there was the promise that he had made to the Holy Club not to marry without their permission. That meant that he needed to get the approval of his brother Charles, among others.

Grace was not happy with John's dillydallying. One of John's helpers, John Bennett, was waiting in the wings for Grace, and he was ready to step in whenever John Wesley's ardor cooled. Prior to Wesley's coming on the scene, it was Bennett who had been Grace Murray's suitor. During a lull in the action, Wesley had entered, center-stage. Bennett was still available.

Some Methodist leaders thought it wouldn't

look right for Wesley to marry Grace Murray. It would look as if she had been his mistress during the past several years of evangelistic forays. Others felt for John to marry someone not of his social class would be a horrible mistake. They thought it would split the movement.

That's when his brother Charles Wesley stepped in. "Jumped in" would be a more accurate phrase. In his opinion, the entire Methodist movement would go down the drain if John married. Any other minister in the movement could marry, but John was a special case. Besides, if John married Grace, Charles thought that half of the leadership would pack their bags. John's diary records his brother's feelings this way: "The thought of marrying at all, but especially of my marrying a servant and one so low-born, appeared above measure shocking to him."

Charles didn't have a moment to spare. Hurriedly, he jumped on his horse and galloped to see Grace. He convinced her that if she went ahead with marriage to John, it "would destroy himself and the whole work of God." Two hours later, he took Grace away, brought her to Bennett, convinced both of them that for the good of Methodism they should marry each other, and in a few days the marriage took place.

John was irate — understandably so. His brother's chicanery was inexcusable. The lifelong close relationship between John and Charles was nearly severed. Gradually, forgiveness came, but not much more. "I can forgive, but who can redress the wrong?" John wrote. Soon, however, John was back on his horse, riding his evangelistic circuit again with the words: "The Lord gave, and the Lord hath taken away; blessed be the name of the Lord."

One biographer doubts that Wesley would ever have married Grace Murray, despite what he had told her: "There can be no doubt that John Wesley delighted to dream of Grace Murray as his promised wife, but in view of his past history, the question arises whether even without Charles' intervention, that promise would ever have become performance."

But fifteen months later, John Wesley did get married, and he was determined that no one would ride off with his bride this time.

One of the few Methodist stalwarts who took John Wesley's side in his disagreement with his brother was Vincent Perronet. Perronet felt that John needed to be married; in fact, he urged it upon him as a duty. At this point, John probably didn't need much urging. Perronet consulted with Banker Ebenezer Blackwell and came up with a candidate, Molly Vazeille, the widow of a London merchant who had left her an inheritance of ten thousand pounds.

With Grace, John Wesley had a checklist to see if his bride-to-be measured up. With Molly, there was no checklist. With Grace, John consulted his brother in advance, and that proved to be a mistake. With Molly, John didn't consult his brother, and that also proved to be a mistake.

He didn't consult with Charles; rather, he told Charles what he intended to do, and he didn't mention the name of his bride-to-be. Charles wrote in his diary, "I was thunderstruck." A few days later when he learned who the woman was, Charles "retired to mourn." He "groaned all the day, and several following ones, under my own and for the people's burden. I could eat no pleasant food, nor preach, nor rest either by night or by day."

Despite his inner turmoil, he dared not intervene this time.

John wasn't going to let a courtship interfere with his preaching schedule, and it didn't slow him down one bit until a fortuitous accident. Crossing London Bridge in mid-February 1751, he slipped and badly sprained his ankle. Despite the pain, he preached on schedule in the afternoon and then hobbled to the home of Widow Vazeille, his fiancée. Molly acted as his nurse for the rest of the week. At her home, he spent the time "partly in prayer, reading and conversation, partly in writing an *Hebrew Grammar* and *Lessons for Children.*"

The conversation with Molly must have settled some things about their marriage. Wesley wanted to make sure that Molly knew he would never touch a penny of her fortune. At least one of her four children was strongly opposed to the marriage, and John probably wanted to remove any suspicion that he was marrying her for her money. No doubt, he also informed her about his evangelistic missions, which kept him away from home 75 percent of the time. She would have her choice of accompanying him on his arduous trips or staying home with her family.

John probably told her, as he had told others, that no Methodist preacher, least of all himself, should "preach one sermon or travel one day less in a married than in a single state." What this meant, of course, was that John would not be making any adjustments to married life; Molly would have to make the adjustments.

The following Monday, his sprained ankle notwithstanding, John and Molly were married. The previous day, Sunday, he had preached on his knees, because he was not able to stand on his sprained ankle. On Tuesday, he was preaching again, once again on his knees. In between he sandwiched in the wedding, and presumably he was married on his knees. We don't know much about his wedding, because he neglected to mention it in his journal.

It was a short courtship, perhaps only sixteen days. And undeniably, it was marriage on the rebound, for John was still smarting from the loss of Grace.

Yet at forty-seven, John had a need to be married. He had always enjoyed feminine companionship, and being attractive to women, he usually had it. But as the Methodist movement grew, he had become more and more isolated in his tower of leadership. Even his brother Charles was now separated from him, separated by the happy marriage that Charles had with Sally Gwynne and separated by Charles' rash action in breaking up John's relationship with Grace. So although he met thousands of people a year and knew hundreds as friends, John was a lonely man at times, and when illness or accident confined him to bed, he was at his loneliest. It was while recuperating that he had fallen in love with Grace. This time he had been confined with a sprained ankle in Molly Vazeille's home on Threadneedle Street in London. The conversation which he enjoyed with Molly in those days of convalescence was delightful. In his words, she gave him "all the assurances which words could give, of the most intense and inviolable affection."

Molly Goldhawk Vazeille Wesley, forty-one, had been a servant girl before marrying a London merchant "who had pampered and indulged her." She had become accustomed to a settled middle-class family life. She had four children, the youngest under five years old. John spoke of her having a "middling understanding," and one biographer speaks of her as being "no more than conventionally religious." Wesley's early biographers denigrated Molly and exonerated John, so some of the early comments on Molly's character may be biased.

Some of these early biographers think that by marrying John, Molly was climbing the social ladder of middle-class respectability and that she inveigled him into marriage, something that Grace Murray and Sophy Hopkey had been unable to do. That is too crass an assessment. Two of her late husband's friends had recommended John Wesley to her. She was flattered by his attention, just as he was pleased with hers. Both of them were ripe for marriage.

The marriage started poorly and went downhill from there. The Sunday after the wedding, John felt he had to explain to his fellow Methodists why he had married so suddenly and had not consulted with his brethren in advance. The explanation confused his brethren and incensed Molly. He spoke of marriage as "a cross that he had taken up" for their sakes and that he had married to "break down the prejudice about the world and him."

Molly was dumbfounded. Was this the man that she had married?

A week later John was off to a conference, then home for a week and then off again on a long road trip in the north. His first day out he scribbled in his diary, "In respect of travelling abroad, the

Methodist preacher who has a wife should be as though he had none." But at night he wrote a warm letter home to Molly, "You have surely a right to every proof of love I can give, and to all the little help which is in my power. For you have given me even your own self. O how can we praise God enough for making us help meet for each other."

John even wrote to his friend Blackwell the banker and asked him to look out for Molly in his absence: "She has many trials; but not one more than God knows and knows to be profitable to her."

Among her trials was John himself. Molly had already gone to Blackwell and complained about her husband's lack of sensitivity to her needs. Then she went to Charles Wesley, only four months after the wedding. It took courage for her to approach Charles because she knew how strongly he had disapproved of the wedding. He agreed to talk to John privately about the problems and then have a meeting among the three of them to engineer a reconciliation. The meeting accomplished little. Molly listed all of the faults, not only of John but also of Charles; John insisted that he couldn't halt his God-given ministry in order to coddle Molly; and Charles felt called upon to recite Latin poetry to calm the waters.

Charles never got along with his sister-in-law. "I must pray or sink into a spirit of revenge," he said after enduring one of Molly's seasons of complaint and insult. Charles' negative feelings were contagious and infected other Methodist leaders. Molly was starting to feel paranoid; she was the wife of the leader of Methodism and yet everyone was against her.

Molly had tried one alternative — staying home while John was on the road — and it hadn't worked. Now she was ready to try the other. If she traveled with her husband, maybe the marriage bond would be strengthened and the negative vibes that she was feeling would disappear.

But it didn't work. Grace Murray had been an ideal traveling companion for John; Molly was not. He didn't want to make the comparison, but he couldn't help it. England's roads were not easy to travel, especially the way John Wesley traveled them. And for one who had a penchant for complaining, Molly found she had plenty to bemoan.

Once again John wrote to his confidant Blackwell: "In my last journey all my patience was put to the proof again and again. I am content with whatever I meet with and this must be the spirit of all who take journeys with me. I never fret. I repine at nothing. I am discontented with nothing. And to have persons at my ear, fretting and murmuring at everything is like tearing the flesh off my bones."

Besides the grueling travel schedule, Molly had to face pouring rain, driving winds, winter cold, stones thrown by angry mobs, and taunts of jeering antagonists. Once, when she arrived at the site of the next meeting, she and John were met by a bevy of adoring women all arrayed in "remarkable neatness." She was conscious of two things: first, that she looked her worst after a fifty-mile ride on horseback and second, that the women were gathered around her husband and didn't care a bit about her. After the meeting, while John was exulting about spiritual blessings, she was complaining about the hard beds, the itchy bed covers that were too small, and the crawly little bugs.

It was no doubt after circumstances like that, that Molly's hair-pulling story took place, if indeed it did take place. According to one of Methodism's traveling preachers: "Once when I was in the north of Ireland, I went into a room and found Mrs. Wesley foaming with fury. Her husband was on the floor, where she had been trailing him by the hair of his head. She herself was still holding in her hand venerable locks which she had plucked up by the roots." Allegedly, this took place about a year and a half after their marriage.

Later biographies partially discredit the story, though they don't discredit it completely. Molly's temper was legendary, and when she lost it, she became quite irrational. John once wrote, in the impersonal way by which he sometimes referred to his wife, "It is a pity. I should be glad if I had to do with reasonable people."

There were occasional respites and at first, John's letters show love and affection. He appreciated her assistance with business and financial matters. He even naively encouraged her to open any letters that came to their home while he was traveling. And when Molly opened some of his mail, it started her off on another tantrum.

The problem was that John's intimate counseling of women did not change after his marriage. He was as warm, loving, and solicitous as ever. So after John and Molly mutually agreed that Methodism's best interests weren't served by her traveling with her husband across the British Isles, she stayed at home, read John's mail, and imagined the worst.

Sarah Ryan, a recent convert and only thirty-three years old, had been appointed by John to be matron of the Kingswood School. She had been married three times without benefit of divorce, and was certainly not the people's choice for the coveted post.

Wesley gave her his pastoral counsel. In his letters to her, he told her his problems with Molly, and the language he used to speak of his spiritual interest in her could easily have been misunderstood. And it was.

In return, Sarah's letters to John said things like: "I do not know how to steer between extremes, of regarding you too little or too much." When Molly ripped open one of these letters, she obviously thought it was too much. What John viewed as *agape* love seemed suspiciously like *eros* love to Molly. She demanded that John stop the correspondence.

"I afterwards found her in such a temper," John writes, "as I have not seen her in several years." And then Molly walked out on him, "vowing she would see me no more."

The temper tantrum and Molly's departure didn't stop John from writing to his female lieutenant at Kingswood. A month later, however, at a meeting that Wesley had with more than sixty of his Methodist ministers and with Sarah Ryan presiding, Molly burst into the room, waving her finger at Sarah and shouting, "The whore now serving you has three husbands living."

After that explosion, Molly returned to John, but as you can imagine, life wasn't any easier. At times, the relationship resembled a pitched battle. Molly was the violent one, John the self-righteous. She accused him of having his brother's wife as a mistress. He accused her of poisoning the minds of the servants against him.

When she refused to give him some of the letters that had arrived in his absence, he broke into her bureau forcibly to retrieve them. When she felt the whole world was on John's side and no one understood her predicament, she doctored some of John's letters to cast them in the worst possible light and then gave them to the London newspapers to publish.

Ebenezer Blackwell, who frequently tried to mediate in the marriage, was sometimes caught in the crossfire. He tried to get John to see that all the blame should not be placed upon Molly. John was angry. He responded: "What I am is not the question, but what she is, of which I must needs be a better judge than you." And "I certainly will, as long as I can hold a pen, assert my right of conversing with whom I please. Reconciliation or none, let her look to that."

In one letter to Molly, John listed ten major complaints, including Molly's stealing from his bureau, his inability to invite friends in for tea, her making him feel like a prisoner in his own house, his having to give an account to Molly of everywhere he went, Molly showing his private papers and letters without his permission, her use of fishwife's language against the servants, and her continual malicious slander.

He vowed that he would be willing to do anything to keep her "in good humor," as long as it didn't hurt his soul or hers or the cause of God. Writing his warm letters to Sarah Ryan and other women was necessary to the "cause of God."

Naturally, John had a problem appearing in public with Molly because he was never quite sure what she would say. He writes that she "could not refrain from throwing squibs" at him and would speak to him as "no wife ought to speak to a husband."

"You violently shock my love," he wrote to her. "You cut yourself off from joint prayer. For how can I pray with one that is daily watching to do me hurt. O Molly, throw the fire out of your bosom."

Molly's problems multiplied. Continually, she

was put down by others in the Methodist move-ment; she wasn't the wife she ought to be for John and she knew it. She was constantly reminded of it. She didn't have John's education, social stand-ing, or stamina; she wasn't suited to be a leader of the Methodist women's bands.

She knew she had an acid tongue. However, not all the blame for their unhappy marriage was hers, and she wanted the world to know it.

She resented the pastoral letters she received from her husband, as if she were no nearer and dearer to him than Sarah Ryan. John would write her: "How do you look back on your past sins?" And "If you were buried just now, or if you had never lived, what loss would it be to the cause of God?" She didn't like to be preached at by her husband.

Besides that, her health was poor. She suffered painfully from gout and had a difficult time going through menopause. She had been defrauded of much of her inheritance and her children had been a concern to her. One had died, another was sickly, and two of her sons proved to be "grievous crosses." John wrote her about these personal problems, suggesting that perhaps these afflictions had come from God "to break the impetuosity and soften the hardness" of her heart. She admitted to herself that this might be so, but she wished that her husband didn't have to keep reminding her.

John Wesley pleaded with her, lectured her and, when that didn't work, he ignored her. John could persuade most women, but he was unable to budge Molly. "One might as well try to convince the north wind," he said.

For more than twenty years, the Wesleys' "marital history pursued its thorny course," writes Stanley Ayling. "A marriage largely nominal and often almost irrelevant; separation frequent, but never final until 1776; perennial mutual resentment."

Sometimes there was a short period of togetherness as in 1766 when Wesley, now sixty-three, wrote, "My wife continues in an amazing temper. Miracles are not ceased. Not one jarring string. O let us live now."

But four years later, on what was almost their twentieth anniversary, Molly walked out again; Wesley's journal records it: "January 23. For what cause I know not, my wife set out for Newcastle, purposing never to return. 'Non eam reliqui; non dimisi; non revocabo.' " ('I have not left her; I have not sent her away; I shall not ask her to come back.')

A year later she came back on her own. Not only did she come back, but she also traveled with him on one of his speaking tours. She was sixty-two at the time.

As they traveled, she felt the strong antagonism of Methodist leadership against her. She felt that they were placing John on a pedestal and her in the gutter. In 1774 she wrote her husband, "For God's sake, for your sake, put a stop to this torrent of evil that is poured out against me."

The torrent did not stop. In 1776 (when he was seventy-three and she sixty-seven) they separated for the last time. "The water is spilt," John wrote. "And it cannot be gathered up again."

Two years later, he wrote her his last letter. It was bitter. "If you were to live a thousand years, you could not undo the mischief you have done." In 1781, at the age of seventy-two, Molly Vazeille Wesley died. She bequeathed nothing to John except her ring. According to the will, the ring was left as a "token that I die in love and friendship towards him."

John Wesley continued his almost herculean labors. He crossed the Irish Sea forty-two times. When he was eighty he conducted a mission tour in Holland. His bitterness against Molly passed away in his final years, and he viewed those stormy years of marriage with the idea that if "Mrs. Wesley had been a better wife," he might have been unfaithful to the great work to which God had called him.

John Wesley was married to his work, and he felt it would have been a grievous sin to be unfaithful to that divine marriage. But sometimes a servant of God fails to distinguish between loving God and loving God's work.

Meet
Jonathan
and
Sarah
Edwards

YOU may remember Jonathan Edwards for three things: (1) he was the preacher of a sermon entitled "Sinners in the Hands of an Angry God," (2) he was a key figure in America's Great Awakening, and (3) he was a brilliant metaphysical philosopher.

None of those things make him a popular folk hero like Johnny Appleseed and none of them give him an inside track on being a good husband.

Maybe he wasn't a particularly good husband; maybe the credit for the good marriage should go to his wife, Sarah.

I'll let you decide that.

In a day when marriages tended to be cold and formal, this one was warm and friendly.

What was it that made this marriage a success?

"A sweeter couple I have not yet seen." That was what Evangelist George Whitefield of England wrote regarding Jonathan and Sarah Edwards.

In fact, after visiting their Massachusetts home for a few days, Whitefield was so impressed with the Edwards' household that he resolved to get married when he returned home to England.

That may sound strange to you. After all, Jonathan Edwards is best known for his fire-and-brimstone sermon, "Sinners in the Hands of an Angry God," in which he says: "The God that holds you over the pit of hell, much as one holds a spider, or some loathsome insect, over the fire, abhors you, and is dreadfully provoked."

Writer Samuel Hopkins visited the Edwards home and had to admire "the perfect harmony and mutual love and esteem that subsisted between them."

Somehow we find it difficult to imagine that Jonathan Edwards could compose one half of such an idyllic marriage. Besides being a revivalist and a theologian, Jonathan was also one of the greatest philosophers America has ever produced. He was a profound metaphysical, abstract theoretician. Does that sound like a person from whose home would come harmony, love, and esteem?

To tell the truth, that home produced not only harmony, love, and esteem, but a study of 1,400 descendants of Jonathan and Sarah Edwards indicated that it also produced 13 college presidents, 65 professors, 100 lawyers, 30 judges, 66 physicians, and 80 holders of public office including 3 senators, 3 governors, and a vice president of the United States.

Much, but by no means all, of the credit for the happy union goes to Sarah Edwards. Elisabeth D. Dodds called her book on Sarah Edwards *Marriage to a Difficult Man*, and no doubt he was a difficult man. Lost in his own world, impractical, and moody, Jonathan Edwards must have been a challenge to live with.

To the outsider, Sarah looked as if she was the one who had it all together. She never seemed to lose her composure, except in times of religious revival. She seemed to manage household and family calmly. But Jonathan Edwards knew better, especially once when she seemed on the verge of a nervous breakdown.

It takes two to make a good marriage, and both Jonathan and Sarah spent time making it work. Both of them were fascinating individuals, so let's take a closer look at them.

On the surface, Jonathan Edwards had a lot in common with John Wesley. Both men were born in the same year — 1703. Both were sons of ministers. Both were raised in remote country towns. Both were surrounded by doting sisters. Of course,

Edwards was born in East Windsor, Connecticut, not Epworth, England, and his father was a Congregational minister, not an Anglican rector.

Jonathan Edwards had ten sisters. All of them were tall — so was Jonathan — and the father called them his "sixty feet of daughters."

A precocious child, Jonathan loved nature and God. At thirteen, he wrote an extraordinary essay on "flying spiders." But even earlier than that he and his playmates had built a hut in a nearby swamp, not as a clubhouse, but as a prayer house. "I used to pray five times a day in secret," he wrote much later, "and to spend much time in religious talk with other boys, and used to meet with them in secret to pray together. . . . I with some of my schoolmates joined together and built a booth in a swamp, in a very retired spot, for a place of prayer. And besides, I had a secret place of my own in the woods, where I used to retire by myself."

He entered Yale to study philosophy when only thirteen. Admittedly, Yale wasn't the university that it is today, but without a doubt Edwards wasn't a typical teenager. Writer James Wood says, "Brilliantly gifted, Jonathan Edwards at the age of fifteen to eighteen could have become a scientist, a naturalist or a philosopher, ranging freely over the whole world of thought. He might well have become a major poet."

Instead, he became a theologian. At seventeen, he was converted. The Scripture verse which God used in his life was 1 Timothy 1:17: "Now unto the King, eternal, immortal, invisible, the only wise God, be honour and glory for ever and ever. Amen." That verse boggled Edwards' mind. After confronting that verse, Edwards says, "I began to have a new kind of apprehension and ideas of Christ, and the work of redemption and the glorious way of salvation by Him."

By the time he was nineteen he had his ministerial degree and was off to New York City for a brief pastorate in a Presbyterian church there.

Then he came back to join the faculty of Yale. It was not the best of times for Yale. Bickering, heresy-hunting, and internal dissension rocked the school. While everyone else seemed to be throwing mud, young Edwards frequently found himself trying to run the college. The task was too big for him. His inadequacy weighed him down. He was beset with "despondencies, fears, perplexities, multitudes of cares and distraction of mind," in his own words.

One distraction was thirteen-year-old Sarah Pierrepont, daughter of a prominent New Haven minister who had been a driving force in the founding of Yale. Sarah was seven years younger than Jonathan and totally unlike him. He was moody; she was vibrant. He was shy; she was outgoing. He was socially inept; she was a natural conversationalist. He was gawky; she was graceful.

And she played "hard to get."

On the social ladder, the Pierreponts were top rung. Her mother was a granddaughter of Thomas

Hooker, noted Puritan divine and New Haven's founding father. Though she was only thirteen, suitors were already standing in line. Almost all of them were more dashing, more suave than gangling Jonathan. And since most girls in colonial days were married by the time they were sixteen, Sarah's single days were numbered.

But she couldn't forget Jonathan. She liked nature and so did Jonathan. They walked and talked along the shore. She liked to read, too. One of her books on the nature of the Covenant deeply influenced Jonathan's theological thinking. He seemed to respect her mind; he liked to talk to her about deep things.

Despite all the pressures and distractions at the university, Jonathan usually had no trouble concentrating. But after he met Sarah, things changed. At the strangest times, she intruded into his thoughts. It took discipline to resist the temptations. He wrote: "When I am violently beset with temptation...[I resolve to do some study] which necessarily engages all my thoughts and unavoidably keeps them from wandering." Such as studying Greek grammar, for instance.

Obviously, it didn't always work. On the front page of Jonathan's Greek grammar book was found this ode to Sarah: "They say there is a young lady in New Haven who is beloved of that Great Being, who made and rules the world, and that there are certain seasons in which the Great Being, in some way or another invisible, comes to her and fills her mind with exceeding sweet delight, and that she hardly cares for anything except to meditate on him.... She has a strange sweetness in her mind, and singular purity in her affections; is most just and conscientious in all her conduct; and you could not persuade her to do anything wrong or sinful if you would give her all the world.... She will sometimes go about from place to place, singing sweetly and seems to be always full of joy and pleasure; and no one knows for what. She loves to be alone, walking in the fields and groves, and seems to have someone invisible always conversing with her."

After three years of friendship and courtship, Jonathan pressed her for marriage with the words: "Patience is commonly esteemed a virtue, but in this case I may almost regard it as a vice."

Choosing the course of virtue, Sarah Pierrepont consented to marry the lanky young man and on July 20, 1727, when he was twenty-three and she was seventeen, they were wed.

They were married for thirty-one years, until death parted them in 1758. Twenty-three of those years were spent in the west-central Massachusetts town of Northampton. Jonathan had been called to take charge of a 600-member parish, stepping into the shoes of his grandfather Solomon Stoddard, who had finally decided to retire at eighty-three. It was the largest and most significant church outside of Boston.

Perhaps the young couple would have been

more suited for a parish in Boston. He was an intellectual, not a frontier preacher. She had come from an aristocratic background and her tastes had been properly cultivated. Yet they felt divinely directed to Northampton.

Jonathan always enjoyed writing more than preaching, so he wrote out all his sermons in the style of the day. His style was certainly not dramatic. According to one biographer, "Tall, slight, round-faced with a high forehead and a student's pallor, he spoke quietly and distinctly. His face was grave, his manner dignified. He used no gestures. He depended for effect on the earnestness of his speech, the clarity of his sentences and the skillful use of the pause." The style was Twentieth-Century Funeral Director.

His sermons, which later became famous, were written on scraps of paper, backs of bills from the general store, backs of his children's writing exercises, and backs of broadside ads. Winslow writes, "Edwards saved scraps of paper just as he saved scraps of time. Both could be made to serve a useful purpose." Today, both sides of Edwards' sermon notes fascinate the historian.

Edwards rose early each day. He noted in his journal, "I think Christ has recommended rising early in the morning by His rising from the grave very early." He had a phobia against wasting time. "Resolved never to lose one moment of time, but to improve it in the most profitable way I can."

But this didn't mean he spent all his time praying and reading his Bible. One hour each day was spent in physical work. Chopping wood was a favorite wintertime chore for him. Sometimes he spent more than that, but Sarah was the manager not only of the household but also of the garden and the fields. Edwards once asked, "Isn't it about time for the hay to be cut?" Sarah responded, "It's been in the barn for two weeks."

Samuel Hopkins wrote: "It was a happy circumstance that he could trust everything to the care of Mrs. Edwards with entire safety and with undoubting confidence. She was a most judicious and faithful mistress of a family, habitually industrious, a sound economist, managing her household affairs with diligence and discretion. While she uniformly paid a becoming deference to her husband and treated him with entire respect, she spared no pains in conforming to his inclination and rendering everything in the family agreeable and pleasant."

Sometimes Hopkins paints a picture of Sarah which is almost too good to be true. Yet when he says that she "conformed to his inclination," he is quite accurate. Edwards occasionally skipped dinner when perplexed by a philosophical or theological problem in his study. At other times he became emotional. "I have had very affecting views of my own sinfulness and vileness; very frequently to such a degree as to hold me in a kind of loud weep-ing so that I have often been forced to shut myself up."

Sarah had to learn to live with that.

Jonathan loved to ride his horse, although he resented the time it took to travel. To make proper use of the time, he wrote notes as he was riding. So that he wouldn't forget his valuable thoughts, he pinned his notes to his coat. When he arrived home, it was Sarah's chore to unpin all the notes and help him sort out the ideas.

To give Sarah some time away from the children, he would frequently go riding with her. It wasn't simply a respite from the cares of the family; it was more the fact that Jonathan enjoyed her companionship. So, about four o'clock in the afternoon, they often went horseback riding together. At such times he would discuss ideas with her and hash over parish problems.

Late at night, when everyone else was tucked in bed, Sarah and Jonathan would share a devotional time together in his study.

The "everyone else" began with a baby girl, born a year after their marriage, and concluded twenty-two years later with the birth of their eleventh child.

"She had an excellent way of governing her children," Samuel Hopkins eulogizes. "She knew how to make them regard and obey her cheerfully, without loud, angry words, much less heavy blows. . . . If any correction was necessary, she did not administer it in a passion. . . . In her directions in matters of importance, she would address herself to the reason of her children, that they might not only know her will, but at the same time be convinced of the reasonableness of it.... Her system of discipline was begun at a very early age and it was her rule to resist the first as well as every subsequent exhibition of temper or disobedience in the child...wisely reflecting that until a child will obey his parents, he can never be brought to obey God."

Jonathan himself set aside an hour at the close of each day to spend with his children. According to Hopkins, the seemingly stern preacher of righteousness "entered freely into the feelings and concerns of his children and relaxed into cheerful and animated conversations, accompanied frequently with sprightly remarks and sallies of wit and humor.... Then he went back to his study for more work before dinner."

A little of Edwards' philosophy about the family is disclosed in his books and sermons. "The whole world of mankind is kept in action from day to day by love." And "Every family ought to be a little church, consecrated to Christ and wholly influenced and governed by His rules. And family education and order are some of the chief means of grace. If these fail, all other means are likely to prove ineffectual."

But despite all that Jonathan may have said about love and joy, it was Sarah who exuded it. When she was gone from the house for a few days, one of Edwards' daughters wrote "all is dark as Egypt."

Visitors came frequently to the Edwards' home and stayed overnight. Usually they were more affected by the character of the home than by anything that Jonathan Edwards may have said to them in conversation.

One visitor named Joseph Emerson commented: "The most agreeable family I was ever acquainted with. Much of the presence of God here."

The first time Hopkins visited, Jonathan Edwards wasn't home. "I was very gloomy," Hopkins recalled, "and was most of the time retired in my chamber." Sarah eventually interrupted and asked about his moodiness. He responded by admitting that he "was in the Christless graceless state," and she talked with him about how he could find the spiritual help he needed. When Jonathan returned, there was more conversation. This combination of Sarah's personal interest, the family atmosphere, and Jonathan's theological explanations changed the course of Hopkins' life.

In 1734, the Great Awakening began in Northampton's church after Edwards had preached a series of expository sermons on love from 1 Corinthians 13. "Scarcely a single person in the whole town was left unconcerned about the great things of the eternal world," said Edwards. He was only thirty-one; Sarah (with four daughters by that time) only twenty-four, and they felt they had a tiger by the tail. Emotions were running wild. Even Sarah herself was caught up in ecstasy. The parsonage had become the most popular place in town. Skeptics who investigated were converted. Edwards tried to impose ground rules to control emotional outbursts, but he wasn't always successful. Some three hundred people claimed to have been converted in the small Massachusetts town during a six-month period.

Just as quickly as it had exploded, it faded away. Then came the letdown. Many of the townspeople who claimed a spiritual experience returned to their old vices. Jonathan was discouraged. What amazed him, however, is what he began to observe happening in Sarah. Normally the cool, calm manager, she began to be irritable, finicky, picky. Looking back on this period in her life, Jonathan later wrote that she was "subject to unsteadiness and many ups and downs...often subject to melancholy. She had," uncharacteristically for her, "a disposition to censure and condemn others."

Of course, an outsider like Hopkins didn't detect any change at first. "She made it a rule to speak well of all," he wrote and lauded her patience, cheerfulness, and good humor. Jonathan knew better.

Opposition to Jonathan Edwards had begun to build in Northampton, and Sarah didn't know how to cope with it. She had always been popular with everyone; she had no enemies, and wouldn't know what to do if she had them. Jonathan, however, had plenty of foes. Even some of his cousins were making life miserable for him. Sometimes he didn't sense the opposition as soon as Sarah did. He stayed in his study. She would be out on the streets, in the shops, meeting people. Clouds were gathering around Northampton. Sarah could often feel what Jonathan could not yet see. She didn't want to disturb him about some of the petty problems in his parish. So she tried to keep up a good front; underneath, however, it was becoming more and more difficult for her to handle.

Sarah was only thirty, but she had already been the lady of the manse for thirteen years when 1740 rolled around. And in the next two years, more seemed to happen than in the previous thirteen.

She had just given birth to her seventh child (and sixth daughter). Four days later, she was shaken by the news that her older sister had died. That spring there was more illness than usual among the children and the financial needs of the Edwards' household became critical. No doubt urged by Sarah, Jonathan went to the town council to ask for a raise in pay.

That fall, twenty-six-year-old evangelist George Whitefield came to town. He had already stirred up Philadelphia and Boston; Northampton, which had experienced an awakening five years earlier, was ripe for another one. So was Sarah. Her heart, she said, "was swallowed up in a kind of glow of Christ's love coming down as a constant stream of sweet light."

No less stirred was Whitefield himself. He was deeply impressed with the Edwards' children, with Jonathan ("I have not seen his Fellow in all New England"), and especially Sarah. He was moved by her ability to talk "feelingly and solidly of the things of God." He was amazed at how much of a helpmeet she was for her husband. Because of Sarah he renewed his prayers for a wife. He was married the following year.

If the Revival of 1735 was Phase One of the Great Awakening, the spark kindled by Whitefield in 1740 was Phase Two. In New England, it was Jonathan Edwards who kept fanning the flames. Though by style and inclination he was an unlikely revivalist, he was called away from home for weeks at a time to conduct evangelistic services in other New England churches. It was during this time that his sermon "Sinners in the Hands of an Angry God" became famous.

During this time, Sarah was once again struggling with her inner stability. She didn't like it when her husband was away from home so much, and yet she knew she couldn't ask him to stay in Northampton. God was using him wherever he went.

Jonathan didn't accept all the invitations that came his way. Some he turned down saying, "I have lately been so much gone from my people." But in mid-January 1742, in one of the most severe winters of the eighteenth century, he was going away again, and Sarah as usual was left home with her seven children. Every even-numbered year since their wedding, a baby had been born in the Edwards' home. In 1742, Sarah wasn't pregnant. "I felt very uneasy and unhappy. . . . I thought I very much needed help from God. . . . I had for some time been earnestly wrestling with God."

Just before Jonathan had left, he had criticized her for being too negative about a "Mr. Williams of Hadley" who had been preaching in Northampton. Her husband's criticism came when she was very vulnerable. She crumbled. "It seemed to bereave me of the quietness and calm of my mind not to have the good opinion of my husband." Not only was she afraid that she had lost the confidence of her husband but she also feared that she had offended Williams.

In Jonathan's absence from town, a recent seminary graduate named Samuel Buell came to the church to preach. Sarah was emotionally down. Of course, she wanted the revival fires to burn through his preaching; yet she feared that Buell might prove to be a better preacher than her husband and in the process show Jonathan up.

Did she want revival to come back to Northampton even if it meant someone other than Jonathan would be God's instrument? Especially if it meant a flashy young preacher like Samuel Buell? It was difficult for Sarah; she struggled for spiritual victory over it. But at length she attended Buell's sermons and "rejoiced" at the "greater success attending his preaching than had followed the preaching of Mr. Edwards."

And then once again Sarah was encompassed with feelings of ecstasy. Her "soul dwelt on high, was lost in God and almost seemed to leave the body." Hymns ran through her mind and she had a difficult time to "refrain from rising from my seat and leaping for joy."

The next day she fainted from exhaustion in the middle of the day, and she "lay for a considerable time faint with joy." During the following days, she says that she had a "sense of the infinite beauty and amiableness of Christ's person, and the heavenly sweetness of his transcendent love." She emerged from the time a renewed peson. "I never felt such an entire emptiness of self-love, or any regard to any private selfish interests of my own. I felt that the opinions of the world concerning me were nothing." From this time on, she experienced "a wonderful access to God in prayer."

While Sarah no longer regarded "the opinions of the world," she did regard the opinion of her husband. And she was afraid that when he returned and found out what had happened, he might think that she had made a fool of herself. After all, he had been trying to keep emotional excesses out of the revival.

But Jonathan's reaction was sympathetic. He was very interested in her experiences and asked her to describe her emotions as carefully as she could. Like a psychologist, Edwards took her stream of consciousness down in shorthand. Later, he published this (though anonymously to keep from embarrassing her) as part of a defense of the revival.

He didn't care to use his wife as a guinea pig or to analyze her experience scientifically, but he felt he had to. He had been disappointed in the seemingly short-lived effects of the revival of 1735. Some people had been genuinely converted, but many had only been caught up in emotion. The question was: What would be the long-range result of Sarah's experience?

He didn't glorify emotional religious experiences — even the experiences of his wife. In almost every emotional experience, "there is a mixture of that which is natural, and that which is corrupt, with that which is divine."

Jonathan, who had observed certain changes in Sarah's cool and collected self in the previous two or three years, could have guessed that Sarah would soon have to have some emotional release for what she had kept bottled up. So part of her experience was natural, but another part of it was undeniably spiritual.

She had been converted as a child; Jonathan knew that. She had lived a good life; Jonathan knew that too. He also knew that this experience was not only emotional; it was also spiritual. Sarah had her thoughts focused on Jesus Christ.

A year later Jonathan wrote up the results of his .

scientific study. Sarah now had an assurance of God's favor that she didn't have before. She was at rest with herself as well as with God. Jonathan was amazed at her "constant sweet peace, calm and serenity of soul." Whatever she did, she was now doing for the glory of God, not for the admiration of men. In Edwards' words, she lived with a "daily sensible doing and suffering everything for God." To him, the "daily sensible doing" was the bottom line of religious revival.

Perhaps, without such a spiritual experience, Sarah couldn't have handled the coming problems in Northampton.

The first problem was finances. Northampton had been growing increasingly unhappy with the need in the Edwards' family for more funds. On the one hand, both Sarah and Jonathan were quite frugal. They saved everything. On the other hand, Sarah had been raised in one of the finest homes in New Haven and it showed. She was accustomed to go "first class." She dressed well and furnished the home in taste. The townspeople didn't understand why Jonathan needed to acquire so many new books. Why couldn't he be content with a few old commentaries? After all, he was preaching from the Bible, wasn't he? The fact that every two years there was another mouth to feed in the Edwards' home didn't get much sympathy. Many families in the area were able to feed several more children on half as much income. History records "a great uneasiness in the town" about the way the Edwards family handled their finances. Finally, Sarah Edwards was asked to turn over the itemized family budget so that everyone could see exactly how they were spending their money.

Why in the world, asked the townspeople, did Jonathan need two wigs? Why did he spend eleven pounds to buy his wife a gold chain and locket? How did Sarah have the nerve to wear such a display of ostentation?

The town was aghast at the extravagance. How could Jonathan ask for more money from the poor church members who were eating off wooden trenchers while he and Sarah and the children were eating from pewter dishes? Jonathan could afford silver buckles on his black shoes, while most of his parishioners had to tie their shoes with common string. And it was obvious to all that Sarah's dresses were expensive.

The financial matter had been a petty irritant for years. When revivals occurred, it was put on the back burner for a while; but the problem was always simmering.

The other problem was that Jonathan had decided not to accept the "non-committed" into church membership. He had discussed it with Sarah and both realized that this would be a major issue. Sarah reported that he "told me that he would not dare ever to admit another person without a profession of real saving religion and spake much of the great difficulties that he expected would come upon him by reason of his opinion."

Why was it such a bone of contention? Because he would be reversing the practice begun by his beloved grandfather, Solomon Stoddard, who had been pastor of the church for more than fifty years. Edwards predicted that, as a result of this decision to reverse his grandfather's procedure, he would be "thrown out of business" and he and his family would be brought to poverty.

Yet Jonathan had to see it through. A college invited him to be its president. Its committee suggested: "You had better run away from these difficulties." According to Sarah: "Mr. Edwards replied that he must not run away."

If the years 1735–1740 were the troubled years for Sarah, the years 1745–1750 were Jonathan's bugbear. Most of his life he had bouts with headaches, colitis, and moodiness. Now he showed his irritation on insignificant matters in the church; even some of his supporters lost heart. A few years later Jonathan mused: "God does not call us to have our spirits ceaselessly engaged in opposition and stirred in anger unless it be on some important occasions." But the issue of a "committed" church membership was important.

In the middle of the unrest, Sarah was asked to go to Boston and take care of an elderly relative who had suffered a stroke. After she had been there a few weeks, Jonathan wrote her tenderly, addressing her as "My dear companion," and told her how the younger children were faring in her absence. Then, after requesting she bring some cheese with her from Boston, he concluded with the line, "We have been without you almost as long as we know how to be."

He often spoke of her as his companion and never did he need a companion more.

In 1750, there were problems aplenty. Sarah had just given birth to her eleventh child and two months later, physically and emotionally depleted, she was flattened by rheumatic fever. That spring, townspeople shunned the Edwards family, refusing to talk with them on the street. Church attendance was only a fraction of what it used to be. A petition was circulated and 200 church members signed it asking for Edwards' dismissal as minister. By mid-year Jonathan was unemployed.

After twenty-three years in Northampton, Jonathan, forty-six, and Sarah, forty, had to move on. The citizens of Northampton, said Paul Elmer More in the *Cambridge History of American Literature*, "had ousted the greatest theologian and philosopher yet produced in this country."

As strange as it may seem, it wasn't easy for Edwards to find another church — or another job of any kind. He was depressed and felt he was over the hill. "I am now thrown upon the wide ocean of the world and know not what will become of me and my numerous and chargeable family." He admitted that he was "fitted for no other business but study."

Northampton, too, had its problems. It couldn't find a minister to fill the shoes of Edwards. For a while, Jonathan filled the pulpit of the church which had boisterously evicted him. He preached without bitterness. Meanwhile Sarah and her daughters made lacework and embroidery and painted fans, which they sent to market in Boston. Those were not easy months for either Jonathan or Sarah.

Then a call came for the distinguished Jonathan Edwards to be a missionary to the Indians in Stockbridge on the western frontier of Massachusetts. There was a small church there. The congregation, composed of several white families and forty-two Indians, was summoned to services by an Indian named David who "blew a blast with a conch shell."

It was a far cry from fashionable New Haven and even from Northampton, the largest church congregation outside of Boston. In primitive Stockbridge, Jonathan preached in a small stuffy room through an interpreter to a small congregation, mostly of Indians who had covered themselves in bear grease as a protection against the winter cold.

Writing to his elderly father in Windsor, Jonathan explained: "My wife and children are well pleased with our present situation. They like the place much better than they expected. Here, at present, we live in peace: which has of long time been an unusual thing with us. The Indians seem much pleased with my family, especially my wife."

Sarah must have wondered about the Lord's leading. Why would He take a scholar like Jonathan and bury him on the frontier? For that matter, why would He take a woman accustomed to the finer things of life and place her in a log cabin surrounded by wigwams?

Actually, Jonathan didn't mind living in isolation from the civilized world. Having a smaller congregation gave him time to do some serious writing. His most famous piece of philosophical writing, *On the Freedom of the Will*, was written in Stockbridge.

Yet it was frustrating to both of them. Jonathan felt inadequate in preaching through an interpreter. He tried to gear his sermons to the level of the Indians, but he realized that there was both a language barrier and a culture barrier between them. Sarah, whose sons and daughters were marrying, found that her interests and concerns were not as much on the ministry at Stockbridge as they ought to be. In Northampton, she had had a ministry of hospitality; the Edwards' home had practically become a hotel. In Stockbridge, not too many New Englanders came calling.

But you couldn't say that things were boring, especially when the French and Indian War started heating up in 1754. Jonathan's mission work was virtually halted. In his congregation had been Mohicans, Mohawks, Iroquois, and Housatonnuck Indians. Some of the Indians favored the French; some the British; and some were on the warpath against both.

Several whites were murdered nearby and soon

the Edwards' home was turned into a little fort. For three years, the Edwards lived in a state of siege. White settlers came from miles away to camp at the compound and four soldiers quartered themselves in the Edwards' house. Later, Sarah submitted a bill to the colonial government for 800 dinners and seven gallons of rum.

Daughter Esther, who had married a young college president named Aaron Burr, returned to Stockbridge to visit her parents during this siege and had trouble getting away again. But while there, she talked to her father about some spiritual problems she was having. "I opened my difficulties and he, as he freely advised and directed the conversation, has removed some distressing doubts that discouraged me much in my Christian warfare. He gave me some excellent directions to be observed in secret that tend to keep the soul near to God as well as others to be observed in a more public way. Oh, what a mercy that I have such a father — such a guide."

It's hardly the picture that most people have of Jonathan Edwards.

The school that Esther's husband served as president was the College of New Jersey, a school that would soon play a part in Jonathan's future. Esther's infant son was named Aaron after his father, and he would play a part — albeit infamously — in America's future.

The French and Indian War finally cooled down, the Indians were returning peacefully to

Stockbridge, and Jonathan and Sarah were ready to resume their missionary ministry, when suddenly they received word that their son-in-law, Aaron Burr, had died.

Five days later, another message came to Stockbridge. The board of directors of the school, which later became better known as Princeton University, had extended an invitation to Jonathan Edwards to replace his son-in-law as president.

Jonathan didn't think he should take the job. Things were just returning to normal in Stockbridge; besides, he had two books on the drawing board that he wanted to finish. Physically and emotionally, he wasn't up to it. "I have a constitution," he wrote back, "in many respects peculiarly unhappy, attended with flaccid solids, vapid... fluids, and a low tide of spirits; often occasioning a kind of childish weakness and contemptibleness of speech, presence, and demeanor, with a disagreeable dulness and stiffness, much unfitting me for conversation, but more especially for the government of a college."

And if that didn't rule him out of further consideration, he admitted that he didn't know algebra and he was not very familiar with the Greek classics. Knowing that a president's job entails much public speaking, he added, "I think I can write better than I can speak."

Princeton's board of trustees was not deterred. They understood his reply to be a "Maybe" rather than a "No," and sent a delegation to Stockbridge to convince the local church council that Edwards was needed in New Jersey more than in Massachusetts' Wild West. Edwards was amazed that his own church council agreed.

So in January 1758, Jonathan left Stockbridge for New Jersey and was inducted as president the following month. His wife, Sarah, would be coming shortly as soon as she was able to conclude the family's affairs in Stockbridge.

But in March, after a presidency of only a few weeks, Jonathan Edwards was stricken with smallpox. As he lay dying, he talked much about his wife and children: "Give my kindest love," he said, "to my dear wife and tell her that the uncommon union that has so long subsisted between us has been of such a nature as I trust is spiritual and therefore will continue forever. And I hope she will be supported under so great a trial and submit cheerfully to the will of God. And as to my children, you are now like to be left fatherless, which I hope will be an inducement to you to seek a Father who will never fail you."

Just before he died, he told one of his daughters who was at his bedside, "Trust in God and you do not need to be afraid."

Sarah, of course, was stunned by the news. What was God's purpose in the call to Princeton? Yet, as Hopkins reported, she "had those invisible supports that enabled her to trust in God."

Two weeks after Jonathan's death, she wrote to one of her children: "My very dear child: What shall I say? A holy and good God has covered us with a dark cloud.... He has made me adore His goodness that we had him so long, but my God lives, and He has my heart."

After thirty-one years of marriage, Sarah was separated from her husband by death. Her favorite verse of Scripture came to mean much more to her at this time: "Who shall separate us from the love of Christ?... For I am persuaded that neither death nor life...nor any other creature shall be able to separate us from the love of God, which is in Christ Jesus our Lord."

Six months later, just as suddenly as her husband had died, Sarah became violently ill with dysentery and died. She was forty-eight.

It had been, as Jonathan Edwards said on his deathbed, a most "uncommon union." One biographer called it "a rare companionship with rich happiness." As companions together, they took time for each other and made their marriage a success. They enjoyed each other's companionship and respected each other's gifts.

Biographers tend to praise Sarah for making the marriage so successful. Perhaps so. But Jonathan shared his ministry with her and thus gave her a larger role than many women of that time enjoyed.

It was an uncommon union indeed.

Meet Dwight and Emma Moody

MANY of you know Dwight L. Moody, the Billy Graham of the nineteenth century. An amazing, seemingly tireless evangelist, he crisscrossed the Atlantic winning hundreds of thousands for Jesus Christ.

Yes, you probably know Dwight L. Moody, but I don't think you've ever heard of Emma Moody, his wife, who liked to stay in the background.

I think you should get to know both of them better. You might be surprised at the kind of man Dwight was at home; you might also be surprised at Emma. Just when you think you have her pegged, you find something about her that amazes you.

But what kind of a marriage would this be — between this Martin Lutherlike man and this "shy and reserved" woman? You might be surprised at that, too.

Do opposites attract?

Can a marriage succeed between people who are so different?

When you get to know Dwight and Emma, you'll discover the answers.

"The only person in all the world who really knew D. L. Moody was his wife," writes Biographer J. C. Pollock.

Maybe that's true, but it is doubtful if anyone — even D. L. Moody himself — really knew Emma Moody.

DL (he seldom used his given name Dwight Lyman) and Emma were opposites. In fact, their son Paul said, "No two people were ever more in contrast. . . . He was impulsive, outspoken, dominant, informal and with little education at the time they met. She was intensely conventional and conservative, far better educated, fond of reading, with a discriminating taste, and self-effacing to the last degree."

It was a good thing that they were different. No home would have been big enough for two people like D. L. Moody.

But don't get the idea that Emma Moody was a pushover. She had a mind of her own.

D. L. Moody never put her in her place; she made a place for herself. It was a behind-the-scenes place that she enjoyed, out of the limelight. For instance, she refused to appear on the platform during her husband's evangelistic campaigns — and she faced criticism for it. Yet early in his evangelistic meetings, she was his prize worker in the inquiry room. "When I have an especially hard case," DL once said, "I turn him over to my wife. She can bring a man to a decision for Christ where I cannot touch him." One of Moody's most famous converts, E. P. Brown, a magazine editor and notorious infidel, was led to Jesus Christ by "shy and reserved" Emma Moody.

Moody's accomplishments as an evangelist on both sides of the Atlantic are legendary. He traveled a million miles, preached to a hundred million people and saw 750,000 respond to a gospel invitation. He revolutionized mass evangelism and founded what is known today as the Moody Bible Institute, the first Bible school of its kind.

A big man, five-ten and more than 250 pounds, he grew bigger and broader over the years of his ministry, not merely in physical size but in the scope and character of his ministry. Emma had a lot to do with that.

Born in Northfield, Massachusetts, in 1837, Dwight Moody had no easy time of it. His father, a whiskey-drinking, shiftless stone-mason, died bankrupt when Dwight was only four. Betsey Moody was left with nine children, including Dwight.

In Northfield, Dwight was exposed to little schooling, little Bible instruction, but lots of hard work. At the age of seventeen, Dwight had his fill of the toil of slow-paced, mundane Northfield and headed for Boston, where he took a job in an uncle's shoe store. He slept in the third floor over the shop. He described it in his almost illegible way: "I have a room up in the third story and I can open my winder and there is 3 grat buildings full of girls the handsomest there is in the city they will swar like parrets." His letter also told how he ate his meals at a hostel "where there is about twenty-five clurks and some girls we have a jolly time." Obviously, Dwight liked girls better than punctuation.

For several months he attended Sunday school at the Mount Vernon Congregational Church in Boston. The class was taught by a dry-goods salesman, thirty-year-old Edward Kimball. One day Kimball visited Moody at work in the shoe store and asked the teenager to come to Christ. Moody responded.

However when he applied for church membership a few weeks later, he was turned down. He didn't have a clear understanding of what salvation was all about, they said.

A year later, discouraged by his church and in disagreement with his uncle who employed him, he packed his bags and hopped an immigrant train (fare $5.00) to seek his fortune in Chicago.

The prospects in Chicago excited him. In letters home, he bragged to his mother, "I can make money faster here then I can in B" (meaning Boston), and wrote to his brother George, "Hear is the place to make the money."

Although he was accepted into membership in a Congregational church in Chicago, he also attended Methodist and Baptist churches. He never worried much about denominational labels. While visiting a Baptist mission, he spotted young Emma Revell — not quite fifteen years old. Emma was teaching a class at the Wells Street Mission; Moody was impressed with both the way she taught and the way she looked. Her hair was black, her eyes dark. She was very feminine and almost quaint. There was a certain elegance about her that impressed twenty-year-old Moody, who was anything but elegant.

He was also not a Sunday school teacher. The Baptists wanted to press him into service as a teacher, but he said he couldn't teach. So instead they gave him the job of going out on the streets and "drumming up scholars," a job that DL did extremely well.

He was also quite successful in getting himself invited to the Revell home where he met Emma's father, Fleming Revell, a shipbuilder of French Huguenot roots who had come to Chicago from London only eight years earlier because he had heard a rumor that Chicago had a future as a ship-building center.

DL liked Emma but not her Sunday school. It was too formal; so in 1858 he began his own. At first it met in an abandoned freight car, then in an unused saloon. Within a year, with DL drumming up the scholars, attendance had grown to 600; in another year it hit 1500.

Teaching a class of Moody's ragamuffins was no picnic, but young Emma was one of his first volunteers. There is evidence that DL enjoyed the companionship of all of his female teaching staff, but Emma became increasingly special to him. In his courtship, DL exercised unusual propriety. He normally brought two other men with him to the Revell home. This was partly because Emma had two sisters, but it was also because DL felt a bit out of place in the more formal atmosphere of the Revell home.

In 1860 they were engaged. DL made the announcement at a meeting of his Sunday school teaching staff. It went something like this: "Up until now, I have always walked all of the girls home, but I can't anymore. I'm engaged to Emma Revell."

Those were days of big decisions for DL. In 1859 at the age of twenty-two, he was making $5,000 in commissions on top of his salary as a salesman. That was in a day when mechanics were making $1.50 a day. DL's goal was to make $100,000 a year, and he doubtless would have made it. Henry

Drummond later declared, "There is almost no question that he would have been one of the wealthiest men in the United States."

But DL was starting to lose interest in money. His Sunday school was taking more of his time and attention. In his spare moments he found himself working with the YMCA. Soon it became apparent that he couldn't stay in business and still do a good job with his Sunday school and the YMCA.

For three months he struggled with the decision. "It was a terrible battle," he said. It would mean delaying marriage to Emma. It would mean sleeping on a bench in the prayer room of the Y and eating cheese and crackers in the cheapest restaurants. (And Moody loved to eat.)

But he finally decided to quit his job. He took a position as visitation secretary of the YMCA. If it paid anything at all, it was a pittance. Marriage would have to wait.

At the outbreak of the Civil War, the YMCA set up an army committee, and Moody was sent to minister to the soldiers. He passed out hymnbooks — more than 125,000 of them — even though he himself had trouble carrying a tune. He went from barrack to barrack, holding as many as ten meetings a night, although he probably wouldn't have called them meetings.

"I saw the dying men — I heard the groans of the wounded," he recalls. He was criticized by Prohibitionists for giving brandy to dying men in order to revive them, so he could tell them about Jesus.

Sometimes they called him "Crazy Moody," because he was always hurrying somewhere. His uncle said, "My nephew Dwight is crazy, crazy as a March hare." His brother agreed, "Dwight is running from morning to night. He hardly gets time to eat."

In fact, he didn't have time for much of anything. "I do not get five minutes a day to study," he admitted, "so I have to talk just as it happens."

He almost didn't have time to get married. But Emma, now a nineteen-year-old school teacher, was still waiting for him. In his biography of Moody, J. C. Pollock writes, "Emma Revell, who had fallen in love with a prosperous shoe salesman, became engaged to a children's missioner, and was now about to marry a six-horse Jehu, wondered where it would end."

They were married Thursday, August 28, 1862. Dwight Moody was twenty-five.

His mother didn't like the idea of her son marrying a girl who had been born in England and who was also a Baptist. Really, she didn't know which was worse.

DL had, of course, told her of the engagement: "I think, dear Mother, you would love her, if you could get acquainted with her. I do not know of anyone that knows her, but that does. She is a good Christian girl."

Since his mother had responded so negatively to the idea of his engagement to this British Baptist, he decided to take his time about informing her of the marriage. Finally, he got around to it two months later. Her reaction was what he expected.

Emma tackled the challenge with her usual calmness. She wrote her mother-in-law: "It makes very little difference to what sect we belong as long as our hearts are right in the sight of God." It took a few more letters and personal visits but Emma and her mother-in-law, Betsey, soon became close friends.

Emma had a way of handling difficult problems. In fact, DL was sometimes unaware of all she was doing. She was practical and orderly. She made her husband eat regularly. She threw away the patent shirts that he boasted "did not need washing for weeks."

She shunned the limelight although her gifts as a teacher were recognized. In Moody's Sunday school she taught a class of about forty middle-aged men.

Once, Moody was escorting a visitor through his Sunday school, and the visitor remarked about the propriety of the situation: "Isn't that lady too young to be teacher of a class of men like that?"

Moody responded that he thought the teacher was handling the class quite well.

The visitor agreed but still insisted that it seemed improper.

Finally Moody said, and rather proudly at that, "That, sir, is my wife."

In the mid-1860s Moody's Sunday school evolved into a church. DL's closest denominational ties were with the Congregationalists, but his church was independent. At Emma's urging, he included a baptistry for immersion as well as a font for infant baptism.

Moody was never ordained as a minister, so other men became the ministers of his church. Yet this didn't keep him from preaching regularly, and there was no doubt in anyone's mind that it was his church.

In his early sermons he emphasized God's wrath. "I preached that God hated sinners, that He was standing behind sinners with a double-edged sword, ready to cut off the heads of sinners," he recalled later. Even Emma said that she sometimes "cringed" at his remarks.

But then the tone of his sermons changed, and it was Emma who was at least partly responsible. Also responsible was a British preacher named Harry Moorhouse, a converted pickpocket.

Moorhouse had been preaching at Moody's church in DL's absence, and when the evangelist returned, he asked Emma how Moorhouse had handled himself. She replied, "He preaches a little different from you. He preaches that God loves sinners."

Moody couldn't understand what Emma was driving at, but she insisted: "When you hear him, I think you will agree with him. He backs up everything he says with the Bible."

From then on, Moody not only preached more on the love of God than on the wrath of God, but also became more of a Bible student; and his sermons showed it.

Emma was also responsible for DL's ministry in the British Isles. After an unusually severe winter of asthma attacks, Emma, only twenty-four, was urged by her doctor to leave Chicago. He suggested that she might go to England where her older sister lived. Always frail, she suffered from recurring headaches and a heart condition as well as asthma. On the other hand, Moody was robust and seemingly tireless. His chief musician, Ira Sankey, once prayed, "O God, tire Moody out, or give the rest of us superhuman strength."

Moody liked the idea of taking his wife to England. He needed a change of pace himself, and besides, he wanted to meet three men that he had admired from afar: George Williams, head of the YMCA; Charles Spurgeon, preacher at London's Metropolitan Tabernacle; and George Muller, who kept the Bristol Orphanage running by his prayer. Whether the trip to England did much for Emma's health is debatable, but it certainly did a lot to open up a new continent for DL's evangelistic ministry.

Emma may not have met all the dignitaries that her husband met, but she met a few unforgettable characters as well. Once as she was traveling alone by train, she happened to sit in a compartment with an insane man. Said he, "Do you know what

I would have done with my wives if I had been Henry the Eighth?" As he talked, he moved closer to her.

Realizing that she couldn't get out of the compartment, the unflappable Emma responded, "No, tell me."

So he told her, complete with all the blood-curdling details of how women could be slain and hinting that he would like to try some of his ideas on her.

Instead of recoiling, Emma said, "You know, I think I could suggest some ways that you have never even thought of." And she tried to top his methods of torture and execution with a few macabre ones that she thought up on the spur of the moment. Eventually, just as her imagination was becoming exhausted, the train pulled into a station and Emma managed to escape.

The story was not surprising to her friends. They had never seen her flustered, and they doubted if even a maniac would raise her blood pressure.

Perhaps if she could keep calm around D. L. Moody, she could keep calm in any kind of circumstances. Moody was always doing the unexpected, acting on impulses, bringing home unusual visitors, and "surging in and sweeping out," as one biographer stated.

When he paused long enough to consider it, DL marveled at the wife God had given him. Once in a sermon Moody stated, "I think my wife would think it a very strange feeling, if I should tell how much I loved her the first year we were married and how happy I was then. It would break her heart."

Publicly, he said, "I have never ceased to wonder at two things — the use God has made of me despite my many handicaps, and the miracle of having won the love of a woman who is so completely my-superior with such a different temperament and background."

By 1871, thirty-three-year-old Moody was very much a family man. Two children had been born into their Chicago home, and some of Moody's rough edges were being smoothed under Emma's gentle sandpapering. At times he was even learning to be courteous. His quick temper was usually kept under control, although occasionally he had to apologize for it in a public meeting.

He was now coming to a crossroads in his career. He had a church in Chicago, a job with the YMCA, and a growing evangelistic ministry that took him away from home for weeks at a time. He felt that God was calling him to more evangelism, but he was resisting.

The Chicago fire burned away his resistance.

On the night of October 8, 1871, the police knocked on the Moodys' door and told them to get out of the area as soon as possible. The city was aflame. Emma calmly wakened her two children and said: "If you promise not to scream or cry, I'll show you a sight you will never forget." She dressed them while they looked out the window at the inferno.

Noticing a neighbor with a horse and wagon, Moody asked if he would take the Moody children to safety. After seeing their children off, DL and Emma packed several Bibles and a few valuables into a baby buggy. Emma tried to get her husband to put a portrait of himself in the baby buggy too. Moody wouldn't think of it. "What would the neighbors say if they saw me pushing a baby buggy down the street with my picture in it?" So Emma carried it herself, under her arm.

For twenty-four hours, DL and Emma didn't know where their children were, or even if they were alive. Emma's jet black hair turned grey overnight.

Chicago was in ashes. So was Moody's church. So was his YMCA. And no longer was there anyone in Chicago from whom he could raise money to build a new church or a new YMCA. So he went to New York and Philadelphia on a fundraising mission. Money came reluctantly.

The problems in raising money to rebuild seemed to verify his call into full-time evangelism, and before long he was headed back to England with Emma, and his two children, Willie, just four, and daughter Emma, now eight. A biographer looking at it psychologically wrote, "When problems began to pile up that were too much for him, he solved these difficulties by getting out and starting anew."

No one in England knew he was coming, except the head of the London YMCA and the doctor at a local lunatic asylum. But the Moodys stayed twenty months and in that time the entire British Isles were set aflame for God.

In Scotland they stayed in the home of Peter Mackinnon, a partner of the British India Line. Mrs. Mackinnon, who became Emma's closest friend, enjoyed both the Moodys. She wrote, "I liked the combination of playfulness and seriousness in Mr. Moody.... He is so simple, unaffected and lovable, plays so heartily with the children, and makes fun with those who can receive it. He is brimful of humor."

As for Emma, Jane Mackinnon wrote, "One day was enough to show what a source of strength and comfort she was to her husband. The more I saw of her, the more convinced I was that a great deal of his usefulness was owing to her, not only in the work she did for him, relieving him of all correspondence, but also from her character. Her independence of thought...her calmness, meeting so quietly his impulsiveness, her humility.... So patient, quiet, bright, humble; one rarely meets just so many qualities in one woman."

Moody's campaigns in the British Isles began with a whimper and ended with a bang. From the tip of Northern Ireland to Cornwall, people were talking about Moody. Emma, in one of her many letters to Moody's mother, talked about him too: "Your son is a gem of a husband."

When the Moodys returned to America, they made their home in Northfield, Massachusetts, where his mother, now in her seventies, still lived. Before long, DL's presence was felt in Northfield.

Concerned about his hometown, Moody prayed for revival there even as he had prayed in London and Glasgow. "The hardest place to begin," he said, "is at home, in your own church, your own family, but that is what God wants us to do."

And that's what Moody did. In the staid Northfield church, he preached one Sunday and saw his own mother stand for prayer. Moody left the platform, sat down in the front pew, his face in his hands, and wept.

Though DL and Emma frequently traveled away from Northfield in the next quarter century, this became their home, and they always longed to get back to it.

The family home in Massachusetts was a beautiful spot, writes James Findlay, Jr., "situated on one of the main roads into Northfield, commanding a sweeping view of the Connecticut River." It was a spacious New England farmhouse, the back portion of which was eventually converted into tiny rooms to serve as a dormitory for Moody's Northfield School.

At home DL relaxed, let his beard grow, wore shabby clothes, puttered in the vegetable garden, and played the role of a gentleman farmer. He loved horses and at one time owned fourteen of them. He cared little for sports and recreation but he enjoyed going out for buggy rides and scaring his passengers out of their wits by the breakneck speeds at which he drove his horses. It was only when Emma was along that he slowed to a respectable speed. He pretended naughtiness and was a "stout and bearded Peter Pan."

Whatever DL did, he did in a big way. When he heard that his mother's chickens had been pecking away in a neighbor's cornfield and the neighbor didn't like it, Moody bought the neighbor's land to keep that problem from recurring. Once when he found himself without a pair of suspenders, he decided to keep that from happening again as well. He went out and bought a gross of suspenders, all white, large-size elastics.

In the homestead, Emma did the canning and made the preserves, visited the neighbors, and entertained DL's friends. She also did most of his correspondence and handled the family finances. DL once declared, "I am not going to give any man ground for saying that we're making a gain out of preaching the gospel." So he turned over the books to Emma.

DL did have a few extravagances. Once he bought a weight-lifting machine which he played with for awhile. He laughed about it later. Indeed, he enjoyed jokes on himself.

Emma managed the house and, in her own quiet

way, the entire family. She took responsibility for the spiritual teaching of their children, catechizing them, memorizing Scripture with them. Though she joined the Congregational Church at Northfield with her husband, she remained a Baptist in her beliefs until her death.

Unlike DL, who didn't read more than he had to, Emma enjoyed reading. As her children were growing up, she studied Latin grammar with them. Later she relearned French.

The one thing that angered Emma was people who took advantage of her husband. A son recalls, "Disloyalty to him was the unpardonable sin in her eyes, unforgivable, unforgettable and above all unmentionable. Here she was implacable."

DL and Emma often took buggy rides together into the woods and hills surrounding their home, and as their son put it, "going where fancy led them, having as it were a renewed honeymoon."

There were times when Moody turned down travel opportunities because "I could not leave my wife." But he did not turn down many opportunities to conduct evangelistic missions. These were often lengthy stays of several months, and usually Emma and the children traveled with him.

Often, they rented a house during the evangelistic missions, but sometimes, they stayed with others. During the Philadelphia campaign they stayed with the Wanamakers. One of the Wanamaker children recalled later, "The thing I remember most was Mr. Moody and father playing bears with us children. Such wild exciting times we had! They could get down on all fours and chase us. We would shriek and scream and run. It was pandemonium." You may be sure, of course, that Emma wouldn't take part in such shenanigans.

Emma wrote to Jane Mackinnon of her daily schedule in the midst of a six-month Baltimore campaign with "Mr. Moody at study and work in the meetings, the children in school, and I in all sorts of work, writing for my husband, attending to some of his calls, and helping him where I can, besides a variety of other things, that don't amount to much and yet make me tired by night."

One of the reasons Emma was getting tired in Baltimore was that she was pregnant. Their third child, Paul Dwight Moody, was born the next spring. He was ten years younger than his older brother, Will.

As the children grew up, both DL and Emma shared a deep concern for them. For instance, when Will began his college work at Yale, DL cautioned him against playing football. "It seems to me like running a great risk of being crippled for life for the sake of a half-hour's fun and exercise," but their greater concern was for the spiritual life of their children. Emma wrote, "If God will only make our children His own, it is the best that we can ask of Him for them." Moody had a special concern because his oldest son, Will, was cool to spiritual matters. Once he wrote Will a revealing letter: "I have not talked much with you for fear I would turn you more and more against Him, who I love more than all the world and if I ever said or done anything unbecoming a Christian father I want you to forgive me. . . . I have always thought that when a mother and father are Christians and their children were not that there was something decidedly wrong with them. I still think so. . . . If I thought I had neglected to do my duty toward my three children I would rather die than live."

Later, it was Emma who wrote to Will about her fear of his "being in college without reliance on the help of Christ. . . . Papa, I know, is praying and I am that God's spirit may lead you to give up yourself to Christ entirely."

The following year Will made a profession of faith. When DL heard of it, he wrote, "I do not think you will ever know until you have a son of your own how much good it did me to hear this."

The younger son, Paul, felt it was easier to confide in his mother than in his father. And Paul gave his mother credit for the success of the home: "If our home seemed so ideal, the secret was my mother."

Emma also deserves some credit for the founding of Moody Bible Institute in Chicago. Moody had served as president of the Chicago Evangelization Society which was planning to launch a training school. But conflict developed between the board of directors and prospective staff members. Moody, who was not on the scene, felt frustrated by the continual bickering. Finally he had enough. He abruptly tendered his resignation as president, a move which would have doomed the entire project. "I am sick and tired of it," he wrote.

When Emma heard about what DL had done, she wrote a nineteen-page letter to the people involved with the Bible Institute, and then got DL to send a wire, withdrawing his resignation.

Soon the Bible Institute of Chicago was launched.

Moody continued his busy schedule, despite his overweight and his advancing age. In one three-month period, he visited ninety-nine places, often speaking three or four times a day. It is said that nothing distressed DL more than idleness.

The year 1899 was difficult for the Moodys. DL was sixty-two and had a full schedule of meetings planned. Two of his grandchildren had died rather suddenly and the parents were suffering emotionally from it. So were the grandparents. DL had been burdened about the city of Philadelphia and had said, "If only it would please God to let me get hold of this city by a winter of meetings. I should like to do it before I die."

So, on his way to an evangelistic campaign in Kansas City, he stopped to visit John Wanamaker in Philadelphia and make final arrangements for a series of revival meetings. He was shocked to find his close friend John Wanamaker living in adultery. He continued to Kansas City, but after two weeks severe chest pains caused him to cease his preaching and he had to return home to

Northfield. A month later, in December 1899, he died.

When DL's body was laid to rest, the spark in Emma's life was gone. She began to fail physically. When neuritis plagued her, she no longer could write with her right hand. So during the last two years of her life she learned to write with her left hand. It was rather typical of the way that Emma Moody handled obstacles.

D. L. Moody once told reporters, "I am the most overestimated person in America." But his wife, he would have said, was the most underestimated. Will Moody once wrote, "Moody found in his wife what he termed his balance wheel. With advice, sympathy and faith, this girl labored with him, and by her judgment, tact and sacrifice, she contributed to his every effort."

An associate of Moody once said, "Only the closest and oldest of his associates knew the extent to which he leaned upon her. She did not intend they should."

Emma supplied what Dwight lacked, and he knew it and appreciated it. She didn't like the limelight; she preferred a behind-the-scenes role. But that doesn't mean she was a nonentity. Far from it. She shaped Dwight both as a man and as a servant of God.

For Dwight, who came from a fatherless home and who didn't know the tenderness of a full family until he met the Revells, it was remarkable that marriage would be so successful. Once again, much credit belongs to Emma.

Dwight needed someone to care for, and Emma, who was physically frail and psychologically strong, was an ideal mate.

In some ways, Dwight was like Martin Luther, impulsive, outspoken and dominant, but with the heart of a teddy bear. But Emma was not a bit like Katie Luther.

Both Martin and Dwight, however, grew in love, appreciation, and respect for the mate God had given. And both Katie and Emma helped shape men who changed the lives of millions.

CHAPTER
FIVE

Meet
William
and
Catherine
Booth

WILLIAM BOOTH reached into the dregs of London's society, preached to the down-and-outers, and organized his Salvation Army. Since then, the Army has marched around the world, ministering mercy and preaching the gospel.

His wife, Catherine Booth, is almost as famous as her general-husband. In fact, 100 years ago, it was a moot point who was the better preacher.

How does a marriage work when both husband and wife are public figures? For that matter, when both husband and wife are strong-minded and frequently dogmatic?

At first, you may wonder how this marriage survived, but soon you will see what both William and Catherine brought to it that made it successful.

I think you'll agree that both William and Catherine are fascinating people. You'll enjoy getting to know them.

It was a big day for William, and it turned out to be much bigger than he could possibly have dreamed.

April 10, 1852, was his twenty-third birthday, and this year it coincided with Good Friday. But that wasn't what made it big.

This was the day when William Booth would become a full-time preacher. Up until this day, he had been a seventy-eight-hour-a-week pawnbroker and a Sunday preacher. Now he was saying farewell to the pawnbroker's shop in south London, where he had slept as well as worked for the past three years.

A businessman had promised him $4.00 a week if he would go full time into preaching. It was not an easy decision and he had struggled with it for months. After all, he was trying to send some support to his widowed mother each week, and that would be hard to do on $4.00 a week. But now the decision was made. He had packed his suitcase and had walked out in the street looking for new lodgings.

Then, unexpectedly he bumped into his businessman friend, who invited him to attend a church service that afternoon. Probably if anyone else had given the invitation, William would have refused it; after all, he had other things on his mind.

Instead, he decided to accept the invitation and go to the meeting. He was glad he did.

Catherine Mumford was also attending the meeting.

They had met a few times before. In some ways they seemed an unlikely couple. He was tall (about six-one), almost Lincolnesque in his appearance, gangling, a bit awkward, sporting a black beard and usually wearing a dark frock coat. She was dark, slightly built, had lustrous brown eyes, and carried herself with obvious refinement.

She had become one of his parishioners at the Walworth Road Methodist Chapel where he frequently preached. One biographer says that "despite their brief acquaintance, a strange affinity had grown up between the tall hollow-cheeked Booth and the dark petite Catherine."

And on this Good Friday that was so significant in William Booth's life, he offered to escort her home after the meeting; she accepted.

Earlier she had admired his preaching (it had "fire" in it); now she began to admire the man. "His thought for me, although such a stranger, appeared most remarkable." She was also impressed with the "wonderful harmony of view and aim and feeling on varied matters. It seems as though we had intimately known and loved each other for years. . . . Before we reached my home we both suspected, nay we felt as though we had been made for each other, and that henceforth the current of our lives must flow together."

Catherine's mother invited William to stay at their home for the night. The next morning when he left the Mumford home, he said he was "feeling wounded." William Booth had fallen in love.

Unfortunately, it was not a good time to fall in love. If it had happened a day earlier when he still had his job, everything might have been different. But now he was a preacher, and $4.00 a week was hardly enough to meet his own bare necessities. He certainly couldn't afford to get married.

Had the decisions of this Good Friday been a mistake?

It would be easy to think so. Both William and Catherine were intense, opinionated, strong-minded, determined. Both were frequently moody and prone to depression.

How could such a marriage work out?

But it did.

Booth lived to see the Salvation Army which he and Catherine began in the London slums spread into fifty-five countries. The merger of social concern and aggressive evangelism among all types of people added a refreshing new dimension to Christendom. No religious movement has ever been more the product of a husband-wife team than the Salvation Army. And no family has ever disseminated the gospel farther and more effectively than

William and Catherine Booth and their eight children.

Perhaps their most serious disagreement during their engagement was over women's equality. She won the argument, but a decade later it was her husband who prodded her into preaching, and a decade after that, she was in more demand as a preacher than he was.

Yes, William and Catherine were an unlikely couple, and both of them came from homes with below-par marriages.

"There is no evidence," one biographer avers, "that Mary (William Booth's mother) greatly loved Samuel Booth (his father), or indeed that she loved him at all. His cold nature and worldly ambitions and his vulgar speech and manners must have checked whatever affection she might have felt for him." His father, whom William himself describes as "a grab-a-get," was a money-minded, small-time builder in Nottingham, who tried to keep up appearances as long as possible but went bankrupt in 1842 when William was only thirteen. That ended William's schooling. His father got him a job as an apprentice to a Unitarian pawnbroker in Goose Gate, Nottingham's slums. Then within a year of his bankruptcy, William's father died, leaving a widow (who tried to eke out a living by selling toys, needles, and cotton), fourteen-year-old William (who had no take-home pay as an apprentice), and three young daughters, one of whom was an invalid.

In the next few years William saw as much of poverty as he ever wanted to see. His family was poor, but working as a pawnbroker, he saw many who were far poorer. He witnessed as poverty-stricken citizens battled soldiers and then broke into bakeries to get bread. He felt the injustice of high taxation and the inequity of the Corn Laws that protected the landowners at the expense of the poor. He even joined a political movement aimed at revolutionizing the British government.

But he also began attending a Methodist chapel in Nottingham. And one night, trudging home after a late meeting, he pondered all the deep thoughts that had been churning through his mind and decided to turn his life over to Jesus Christ. Undramatically, William Booth had become a Christian.

Six years later, having finished his appointed time as an apprentice, William tried to find a job, preferably at something unrelated to pawnbroking. But he was unsuccessful. After a year of unemployment in Nottingham, he decided to move to the big city of London. Those twelve months of unemployment were "among the most desolate of my life," William recalled later. "No one had the slightest interest in me."

London didn't seem much better than Goose Gate in Nottingham. If anything, the poverty was worse. Jobs were just as scarce. And the city, as William quickly discovered, literally stank. Smoke from three million chimneys blended in a putrid amalgam with gin, onions, dung, drying batter, and sewage. The River Thames had been appropriately nicknamed "The Great Stink."

Because he could find nothing else, he finally accepted work as a pawnbroker, a job that he was ashamed of for the rest of his life. His one joy in life came on Sundays when he often took the opportunity to preach, sometimes outdoors in a London park and sometimes in a small chapel eight miles away. It was a long walk.

He regretted he couldn't spend more time preaching, but that was impossible. "There is no way; no one wants me."

After all, the Methodists had just declined to renew his church membership (he had stubbornly refused to give up his open-air preaching in Kennington Common), and his application to serve as chaplain on a convict ship bound for Australia — a job hardly any self-respecting minister wanted — had been rejected. Besides that, a doctor had warned him that he was such a bundle of nervous energy that he probably wouldn't live too long. And now he was having increasing stomach problems and was rapidly developing ulcers.

So just as he was about to give up on everything, he met this businessman "angel" who wanted to enlist him as a minister with a group which had broken with the Methodists. Shortly thereafter, he met Catherine.

Catherine's mother was rigid, narrow, and sometimes neurotic. Her father was a backslidden

Methodist minister turned coachmaker, for whom both mother and daughter prayed. For a while he was active in the temperance movement, but eventually took to drink himself.

William Booth once said that Catherine's mother was "a woman of the sternest principle he had ever met. . . . To her, right was right no matter what it might entail." She refused to allow her daughter to study French because it might open the door to French novels and infidel literature. Most of Catherine's education was at home, because Mrs. Mumford was afraid of the companions with whom her daughter might have to mix at school. To avoid secular contamination, Catherine grew up without playmates. Instead she played church with her dolls and often preached to them. Table conversation was always adult and serious. The only other child in the family, a brother, left home as soon as he could (at age sixteen) to sail to America, and that left Catherine to be her mother's confidante.

Nervous and delicate, Catherine battled various health problems from childhood. When she was fourteen, curvature of the spine forced her to be bedridden for several months; when she was eighteen, tuberculosis forced her to leave home for the seashore town of Brighton for sixteen months. She returned to London from her convalescence about the time that William Booth came to London to hunt for a job.

It was said of Catherine: "Next to religion, she cared most for disputation." Strangely enough, that endeared her to William. He had never met anyone like her.

She had definite thoughts on almost everything, even as he had. She even had definite thoughts on the kind of man she wanted to marry. He would have to have religious views similar to hers; he would have to be a man of sense and character ("I could never respect a fool"); and he would have to have similar tastes. She also believed she must be physically attracted to him. Lastly, he must be a total abstainer. Besides that, she had a personal preference for a minister. William Booth met all the qualifications except for not being a total abstainer. She soon convinced him of the importance of total abstinence, and that made him her perfect match.

Within a month of their Good Friday tryst, Booth began having second thoughts about many things. People didn't seem to respond to his preaching; denominational officials were giving him the cold shoulder; congregations appeared to be so much better educated than he. Maybe he should return to pawnbroking so he and Catherine could get married. He shared his thoughts with Catherine.

In a "My dear friend" letter, she responded, "Never mind who frowns, if God smiles. The words, 'gloom, melancholy and despair,' lacerate my heart. Don't give way to such feelings for a moment. God loves you. He will sustain you. . . . The thought that I should increase your perplexity and cause you any suffering is almost unthinkable. I am tempted to wish that we have never seen each other. Do try to forget me."

William misunderstood the letter. He thought she was rejecting him, and dashed off a frantic note in response. She wrote back: "I fear you did not fully understand my difficulty. If you are satisfied that the step is not opposed to the will of God, let us be one, come what may." A few days later they were engaged.

The engagement came easily, compared to the marriage. Their wedding would have to wait for more than three years.

On the night of their engagement Catherine wrote: "The evening is beautifully serene and tranquil, according sweetly with the feelings of my soul. The whirlwind is past and the succeeding calm is in proportion to its violence. All is well. . . . The more you lead me up to Christ in all things, the more highly shall I esteem you; and if it be possible to love you more than I do now, the more I shall love you."

Because William traveled a great deal in the next three years, the correspondence of the engaged couple continued. His notes were short; hers were frequently twenty-five hundred to three thousand words in length. One biographer referred to them as "Puritan love letters." Perhaps, but there was also plenty of emotional warmth conveyed in them.

He spoke of his problems: "I walked eight miles yesterday. I ought to have ridden. I feel uncommonly tired and weary this morning. My head aches and I feel altogether out of order."

In her responses, she sometimes scolded him: "Don't sit up singing till twelve o'clock after a hard day's work. Such things are not required by either God or man, and remember you are not your own."

Sometimes she sounded schoolmarmish: "Try and cast off the fear of man," but soon she would sound human again: "You may justly consider me inadequate to advise you in spiritual matters, after living at so great a distance from God myself."

She knew that she shouldn't worry about him, but she did anyway. "The very fact of loving invests the being beloved with a thousand causes of care and anxiety, which, if unloved, would never exist. At least, I find it so."

Biographer William Nelson wrote, "It would never have done for a half-hearted man to have married Catherine Mumford." Some of her letters would have intimidated a lesser man. Once, she wrote, "I ought to restrain the tide of feeling more than I do in writing to you," but she said that she did not want to "cool or restrain it, so that you may know of what I am made."

She was not afraid to give him her pastoral advice: "I want you to be a man and a Christian and then I am satisfied. . . . I have such views of what the man must be to whom I give myself that it would be bitterer than gall to find myself bound to one in mind and head manifestly unworthy." Perhaps she was thinking of her parents' marriage, and a father who had lost interest in spiritual matters. "God is not glorified so much by preaching or teaching or anything else as by holy living."

Their marriage was delayed by financial reasons, but there were other problems as well. Booth couldn't find a congenial denomination. Before their engagement, both of them had left the Methodist Church (or were asked to leave) and had joined the Methodist Reformers. However, there was much bickering among the Reformers, and the lay leaders were vying with the clergy for power. So the young couple withdrew from the Reformers. Catherine began attending a Congregational Church and encouraged William to study for the Congregational ministry. But the books they gave him to read were too Calvinistic to fit his personal theology. William and Catherine didn't know where to turn until another small Methodist splinter group invited William to take a circuit of churches about one hundred miles north of London. Though it meant parting from Catherine, it was an opportunity he could not pass up.

One of his letters to Catherine describes his feelings: "I am still whirling about the country. Tonight I go back to Spalding; Tuesday to Rinchbeck; Wednesday to Suttleton; Thursday a special ser-

140

mon at Boston. . . . I wish all this writing was at an end and that you were here, mine, in my arms, and yet I cannot help having fears and doubts about the future. How I wish the Reformers would amalgamate with the New Connexion or with the Association and that all this agitation were ended. . . . But I am always running before to find doubts and fears; mine has always been a restless and dissatisfied life, and I am fearful that it will continue so until I get safe to heaven."

In his restlessness he even thought of going to the United States and trying to become a Methodist preacher there. He asked Catherine if she was willing to go with him. She assured him that she was, but she cautioned him, in one of her more pastoral letters, against "ambition." "I see ambition to be your chief mental besetment. . . . Ambition even to save souls may not be sanctified. But ambition simply to glorify God, the soul risen up to the one sublime idea of glorifying God, must be sanctified."

While William was worrying, Catherine was preparing — preparing to be a minister's wife. "I enlarged the scope of my reading, wrote notes and made comments on all the sermons and lectures that appeared at all worthy of the trouble, started to learn shorthand. . . ."

The hardest thing for her to learn was the piano. William felt strongly that every minister's wife should play the piano, so she tried to learn. But it didn't come easily for Catherine. She lacked any musical sense. It was hard on her nerves; it made her irritable. She wrote: "Patience is a thing I am very deficient in. The music has tried me almost beyond endurance. I could freely abandon it and touch it no more. Once today I raised my eyes from the music and through some bitter tears looked at your likeness and said to myself, 'William, I do this for thee.' So I will persevere and I will for your sake go on. Measure my love for you by this standard."

What came easier for Catherine was writing sermons and outlines for her husband-to-be. He was so busy traveling from one of his circuit churches to another that he often dashed off notes to her such as "I want a sermon on the Flood, one on Jonah, and one on the Judgment. Send me some bare thoughts; some clear, startling outline. Nothing moves people like the terrific. They must have hell-fire flashed before their faces or they will not move."

Catherine obliged, although she occasionally reminded him to "watch against mere animal excitement in your revival services. . . . I never did like noise and confusion, only so far as I believed it to be the natural expression of deep anxiety wrought by the Holy Ghost; but my love, I do think noise made by the preacher and the Christians in the church is productive of evil only. I don't believe the Gospel needs such roaring and foaming to make it effective, and to some minds it would make it appear ridiculous, and bar them against its reception forever."

Catherine developed four rules for their future married life: (1) Never to have any secrets from my husband; (2) Never to have two purses; (3) Talk out differences of opinion to secure harmony and don't try to pretend the differences don't exist; (4) Never to argue in front of children.

The fact that two of the four had to do with differences of opinion underlines the fact that they were both opinionated people.

One area where they initially differed regarded women. He felt that a woman has more in the heart but a man has more in the head. Strongly disagreeing, she said that she would never marry a man who would not give to woman her proper due. She acknowledged that because of "inadequate education" most women were "inferior to man intellectually. . . . But that she is naturally so, I see no cause to believe."

William seemed to delight in the correspondence. Once he wrote: "I want you to hear me, to criticize me, to urge me on. I feel such a desperate sense of loneliness, so oppressive to my spirit. I speak and preach and act, and it is passed over; there is one with whom I can talk over my performance; to others I cannot mention it for fear of being thought egotistic or seeking for praise, and for some reasons others say little or nothing of it to me." Catherine never seemed reticent to speak out.

At times during the long engagement, Catherine seemed almost too willing to see the marriage postponed. Perhaps she enjoyed the intellectual intimacy more than she might the physical intimacy. But when he became discouraged, she talked radiantly about their future life together: "We will make home to each other the brightest spot on earth; we will be tender, thoughtful, loving and forbearing. . .yes, we will."

After a year on the Spalding Circuit, one hundred miles north of London, William joined another Methodist splinter group called the New Connexion and returned to London for six months of study. Catherine had encouraged him to make the move even though ministers had to wait four years before they were free to marry. William could hardly endure six months of schooling while thousands were dying and going to hell; and he didn't think much of the four years' probation before marriage either.

Fortunately, his tutor was lenient and allowed William to do more preaching than classroom study; also it was fortunate that the New Connexion made a special exception in William's case and agreed to let him get married after a probation of only one year.

Early in 1855, not quite twenty-six years old, William became an evangelist with the New Connexion. Once again as he was frequently separated from Catherine, he became depressed and lonely. He wrote her: "You know me; I am fitful, very; I mourn over it, I hate myself on account of it. But there it is; a dark column in the inner life of my spirit. You know it." Despite his depression, during four months of evangelistic efforts, he saw 1739 people profess decisions for Jesus Christ.

In June, William and Catherine, now both twenty-six, finally got married. It was a small and simple wedding with only her father, his sister, and the presiding minister present. After a one-week honeymoon, they left for his next evangelistic foray.

She wanted to accompany him everywhere — for his sake as well as hers — but her health couldn't take it. When Booth left her in London once, she wrote, "I feel as if part of myself were wanting."

A few months later she wrote her parents: "He is kinder and more tender than ever. Bless him! He is worth a bushel of the ordinary sort."

After eight months of an itinerating marriage, she wrote a letter to a friend, extolling her husband's preaching: "My precious William excelled himself and electrified the people. You would indeed have participated in my joy and pride could you have heard and seen what I did. Bless the Lord, O my soul."

The next paragraph was written with a bolder, less refined penmanship. "I have just come into the room where my dear little wife is writing this precious document and snatching the paper have read the above eulogistic sentiments. I just want to say that this very same night she gave me a curtain lecture on my blockheadism, stupidity, etc., and lo, she writes to you after this fashion. However, she is a precious, increasingly precious treasure to me, despite the occasional dressing down that I come in for."

Undaunted, Catherine resumed the letter in the next paragraph. "We have had a scuffle over the above, but I must let it go, for I have not time to write another, having an engagement at two o'clock, and it is now near one. But I must say in self-defense that it was not about the speech or anything important, that the said curtain lecture was given, but only on a point, which in no way invalidates the eulogy."

William loved his evangelistic work, but for one reason or another his fellow ministers in the New Connexion were not always as enthusiastic. So in 1858, after three extremely busy and successful years of evangelism, the Booths were assigned to a small ninety-member charge. But this small parish gave Catherine the opportunity to do some preaching herself.

When a nearby minister attacked women's right to preach, Catherine responded with a thirty-two page rebuttal. To her mother she wrote: "Would you believe that a congregation half composed of ladies could sit and hear such self-depreciatory rubbish?"

Despite the fact that William was "always pestering me to begin," Catherine had personally been timid to speak in public. But in 1860, after the birth of daughter Emma, she felt "divinely compelled" to say something in a church service. She said that she heard the devil telling her, "You will look like a fool." In reply, she said, "I have never yet been a fool for Christ. Now I will be one."

The personal word that she gave at the conclusion of the morning service was so well received that she was asked to speak in the evening. That began a speaking ministry in which she often was better received than her husband.

What made this remarkable, says author Richard Collier, was "Most Victorian women lived in a world of sandalwood fans, white kid-gloves and tortoise-shelled card cases; a respectable woman who raised her voice in public risked grave censure."

An article in *The Gospel Guide* described Catherine's style: "In dress nothing could be neater. A plain, black straw bonnet slightly relieved by a pair of dark violet strings; a black velvet loosely-fitting jacket, with tight sleeves, which appeared exceedingly suitable to her while preaching, and a black silk dress, constituted the plain and becoming attire of this female preacher. . . . Her delivery is calm, precise and clear without the least approach to formality or tediousness."

She never could understand why reports on sermons by women preachers seemed to concentrate more on fashion than on content.

Each year for four successive annual conferences, William waited for the New Connexion to reassign him back to evangelistic work. He felt he had been divinely called to evangelism and that the denomination was resisting the will of God. He couldn't understand why they didn't allow him to be an evangelist.

Catherine urged him to leave the denomination; William was cautious. He had a conservative streak. Catherine explained: "I do not see any honorable course for us but to resign at once, and risk all. But William is afraid. He thinks of me and the children; and I appreciate his loving care, but I tell him God will provide."

After the denomination's 1861 conference, the Booths left. With four young children and with no visible means of support, they stepped out in faith. To help with the finances, Catherine with almost too much willingness sold her piano. For the next four years, William, sometimes with Catherine by his side, conducted evangelistic missions up and down England.

Frequently Catherine had to stop to have a baby or to restore her health or to stabilize her young family; William had his ups and downs as well.

Once when Catherine was back in London he wrote her: "I have not been in very good spirits today. I have been looking at the dark side of myself. In fact, I can find no other side. I seem to be all dark, mentally, physically, spiritually. The Lord have mercy on me! I feel I am indeed so thoroughly unworthy of the notice of either God or man."

He was a man of moods. "On bad days, he grew tense and irritable," writes one biographer, "and his children learned to make themselves scarce. Only with Catherine did Booth all his life preserve the lover's tenderness."

His relationship with Catherine was unique and he knew it: "I am quite sure," he wrote her, "that we do now realize far more of this blissful union, this oneness, than very many around. I meet with but few who think and love and hate and admire and desire alike to the same extent that we do, and also with very few who realize as much domestic and conjugal felicity."

But after bearing six children in nine years, struggling with a wandering, homeless existence, facing recurrent health problems, and trying to cheer up William, Catherine became depressed herself. During this time she wrote, "I know I ought not to be depressed. I know it dishonors the Lord. But I cannot help it. I have struggled hard, more than anyone knows, for a long time against it. Sometimes I have literally held myself head and heart and hands, and waited for the floods to pass over me. Well, at present, I am under, under, under."

Her youngest baby was suffering from convulsions; she was having trouble paying the bills; she had her hands full with an active brood of children; and her spinal problems seemed to be returning. Meanwhile, William was caught up in the emotional excitement of successful revival meetings in northern England. So he wrote her: "Cheer up. All will be well. Whatever you do, don't be anxious."

He also advised her to seek some diversion. Not long afterwards, she received an invitation to conduct revival meetings herself, entirely apart from her husband, in south London. William encouraged her to accept the invitation and she did.

The meetings were so successful that they led to more invitations in other parts of London. Soon her husband came to London to join her.

She spoke to two to three hundred prostitutes at a meeting of the Midnight Movement for Fallen Women while William invaded the most neglected and underprivileged sections of the poverty-ridden city. Then came another turning point for the Booths.

"I remember it well," Catherine recalled. "William had come home one night tired out as usual. It was between eleven and twelve o'clock. Flinging himself into an easy chair, he said to me, 'Oh Kate, as I passed those gin palaces tonight I seemed to hear a voice saying, "Where can you go and find such heathen as these, and where is there so great a need for your labor?" '

"I remember," she added, "the emotion that this produced in my soul. This meant another start in life."

It also meant more financial problems. On the plus side it meant for Catherine a permanent home at last. And more importantly, it meant the launching of the East London Mission which gradually evolved into the Salvation Army.

The process wasn't easy.

As one author puts it, "This delicate and ill-educated man, married to a very sick woman, stood by himself on Mile End Waste and was pelted with garbage by the drunkards who reeled out of their gin palaces to deride and mock him."

William took his oldest son, Bramwell, into an East End pub and showed him the world of drunken women and violent men. Then he told his son, "These are our people. These are the people I want to live for and bring to Christ."

At home, however, William wasn't easy to live with. Perhaps he needed a place where he and Catherine could be alone without the children. His stomach problems caused him to be irritable and harsh-tempered. Undoubtedly he loved his children, but his love often came through more clearly from a distance. They got on his nerves. "His kisses," one writer says, "were more on paper than on their lips."

Biographer Begbie alleges that William was fond of his children, but was "too absorbed by his work, too distracted by anxieties, and too often tired by physical pain to give them the whole and perfect love of a father's heart."

He had a fetish for cleanliness and punctuality, and his children were whipped if they stepped out of line. Though he didn't take the title of the General of the Salvation Army until the late 1870s, he was already a general at home.

In 1868 Catherine gave birth to her eighth child, the last of the amazing brood of Booth children. In time all of them not only made their personal confessions of faith but also became active in the ministry. When he was sixteen, Bramwell was placed in charge of five Food-for-the-Million shops where the poor could buy food cheaply; by the time he was twenty, he was appointed as his father's Chief of Staff. Their second son, Ballington, was placed in charge of a training home for men when he was only twenty. Their oldest daughter, Katie, began preaching on the streets when she was only sixteen.

Once when she was asked the secret of raising a Christian family, Catherine responded: "The very first principle is that you acknowledge God's entire ownership of your children."

Each year the work increased. By 1870, there were a dozen preaching stations, besides evening classes, Ragged Schools, reading rooms, Penny Banks, Soup Kitchens, and Relief of the Destitute and Sick Poor, not to mention a new magazine (with occasional articles from Catherine as well as William) which eventually became known as the *War Cry*.

As the work grew, it took over their home. Even bedrooms doubled as offices. Catherine's only relief came when she was able to induce a friendly builder to put in a double ceiling packed with sawdust over a small sanctuary that she had. Later Catherine wrote: "From the attic to the kitchen every available scrap of space has been occupied with correspondence and secretaries. . . . The pressure upon the General and on my children was always so severe that, after putting in a good day's work, it seemed as if still more remained to be done, and so they would sit up over them til the small hours of the morning. . . . Only too glad would I have been if I could have retired to some little cottage corner where I could have buried myself in the privacy which, the more I loved, the less I seemed able to obtain."

Despite the rapid growth of the movement, the Booth family continued to flirt with bankruptcy. Somehow, Catherine, besides preaching and teaching and struggling with increasing health problems, had the reputation of being a good homemaker as well. In later years, their eldest son, Bramwell, described his mother this way: "She not only patched our clothes, but made us proud of the patches." A visitor who stopped in for tea was surprised to find Catherine darning her husband's socks.

Yet Catherine continued to be as strong-willed as ever. Sometimes she and William would dogmatically argue opposite points of view one night; then having been convinced by the other's arguments, each would switch and argue the opposite side the next evening. Early in their marriage, Catherine seemed to caution her husband against emotion in revival meetings; later in their married lives, they seem to have changed sides. Catherine's views on "holiness" teaching were always stronger than those of her husband, and from the start she opposed the administration of the sacraments (partly because she opposed giving wine to former alcoholics) while he took longer to make up his mind on the subject.

They also had an understandable disagreement when the brewers of London donated money to the Salvation Army. She wanted to send it back. His arguments prevailed. He argued that it was better to keep it and undo some of the mischief the brewers had done.

Financial pressures never let up. Earlier, she had been the optimist and he the pessimist; now the roles reversed. The continuing financial burdens weighed on her. "My precious husband is careworn and overwrought with this great work," she wrote in a letter. "The tug to get money — that is bad enough, but to have to think of self is worse than all.

"You will say, 'Where is your faith?' I fear it is very low. Yet I do hold on to the promises. I believe in some way the Lord will deliver us.... It seems very strange that the greatest abundance seems to go where they know least how to use it."

Then when William got gastric fever, a daughter got smallpox, and Catherine herself became ill again, depression returned: "My soul seems dumb before the Lord. A horror of great darkness comes over me at times. But, in the midst of it all, I believe He will do all things well."

It was in 1888 when the Booths were nearly sixty and the Salvation Army had become international with their children spreading the message into distant lands, that Catherine discovered a small cancerous growth on her breast. She was given about eighteen months to live.

She told her husband: "Do you know my first thought? My first thought was that I regretted that I should not be here to nurse you when you came to your last hour."

It was a crushing blow for William. He wrote in his diary: "I am sixty years old, and for the first time during all these long years, so far as memory serves me, has God in His infinite mercy allowed me to have any sorrow that I could not cast on Him." He could not understand it.

He spoke of one night when during "the great part of the night I had a strong conflict myself with the enemy, and great darkness and heaviness in my heart.... Life became a burden, almost too heavy to be borne."

Later he wrote: "To stand by the side of those you love and watch the ebbing tide of life, unable to stem it or to ease the anguish, while the stabs of pain make the eyes flash fire and every limb and nerve quivers, forcing cries of suffering from the courageous soul — is an experience of sorrow which words can but poorly describe."

During the months of her illness, she said she felt as if she were "dying in a railway station." It certainly seemed like it. Urgent telegrams came at all hours day and night. Lieutenants barged into the house reporting to General William or to Chief of Staff Bramwell. William or Bramwell was always leaving or returning on some Army business.

And Catherine herself was still deeply involved. For several months she continued preaching. When she became too weak to do more, the action came to her. Richard Collier writes in *The General Next to God*, "Her bedroom was the conference room where the finite points of the Army's expanding social policy were now argued and shaped."

Of course, William kept busy. As the months of her illness dragged by, he stayed closer to home. He was trying to keep his mind on writing a book, but it wasn't easy. Sometimes he would break down in tears, moaning, "How can it be? How can it be?"

But he continued to arise daily at six A.M. for a cold bath and two hours work before breakfast, which was often a boiled egg, buttered toast, and unsweetened hot tea.

It was amazing how rapidly the Salvation Army had grown. By 1890, there were 2,900 centers; about $50 million had been raised for the under-privileged; 10,000 Salvation Army officers were holding 50,000 meetings each week.

By this time, Catherine had a notable surgeon tending to her, Sir James Paget. She finally consented to surgery, but now it was too late. By 1890, Catherine had come to the end. She could no longer speak, so she pointed to a wall motto above the mantel, which said, "My grace is sufficient for thee."

After Catherine's death, the Army continued to flourish, but the close-knit Booth family started to unravel. Catherine was the one who had always held the strong-willed family members together. "I am your General first and your father afterwards," William told one daughter. Although they remained in Christian work and their zeal for God continued, six of the eight children eventually defected from the Salvation Army. With their defection, they also became estranged from their father.

One son who remained faithful to the Army and to William was Bramwell, his Chief of Staff. To him, William paid the highest compliment, "You are like her, Bramwell, your Mother."

When you put together two determined people like William and Catherine, both of whom came from problem marriages, you wouldn't expect to find the love and commitment that was evidenced by the Booths. They needed each other. At times they admonished one another; at other times, they propped each other up. The fact of the matter is, they loved each other.

It's an unusual army that is founded in love, but, of course, the Salvation Army has always been an unusual army.

BIBLIOGRAPHY

THE LUTHERS
Bainton, Roland. *Here I Stand*. Nashville: Abingdon Press, 1950.
D'Aubigne, J.H. Merle. *The Life and Times of Martin Luther*.
Chicago: Moody Press, 1950.
Friedenthal, Richard. *Luther: His Life and Times*. New York:
Harcourt, Brace, Jovanovitch Co., 1967.
Luther, Martin. *Table Talk*. New Canaan, CT: Keats Publishing
Co., 1979.
Schwiebert, E.G. *Luther and His Times*. St. Louis: Concordia
Publishing House, 1950.

THE WESLEYS
Ayling, Stanley. *John Wesley*. Cleveland: Collins-World, 1979.
Brailsford, Mabel. *A Tale of Two Brothers*. New York: Oxford
University Press, 1954.
Flint, Charles. *Charles Wesley and His Colleagues*. Washington,
D.C.: Public Affairs Press, 1957.
Lee, Umphrey. *The Lord's Horseman, John Wesley the Man*.
Nashville: Abingdon Press, 1954.
Wesley, John. *The Heart of Wesley's Journal*. New Canaan, CT:
Keats Publishing Co., 1979.

THE EDWARDS

Dodds, Elisabeth D. *Marriage to a Difficult Man*. Philadelphia: Westminster Press, 1971.

Hitt, Russell T., ed. *Heroic Colonial Christians*. Philadelphia: J.B. Lippincott Co., 1966.

Miller, Perry. *Jonathan Edwards*. Westport, CT: Greenwood Publishers, 1949.

Winslow, Ola Elizabeth. *Jonathan Edwards*. New York: Macmillan Publishing Co., 1947.

Wood, James Playstead. *Mr. Jonathan Edwards*. New York: Seabury Press, 1968.

Wright, Elliott. *Holy Company*. New York: Macmillan Publishing Co., 1980.

THE MOODYS

Bradford, Gamaliel. *D.L. Moody, A Worker in Souls*. Doran and Company, 1927.

Curtis, Richard K. *They Called Him Mr. Moody*. Garden City, NY: Doubleday & Co., Inc., 1962.

Findlay, James J., Jr. *D.L. Moody, American Evangelist*. Chicago: University of Chicago Press, 1969.

Moody, Paul D. *My Father*. Boston: Little, Brown & Co., 1938.

Moody, William R. *The Life of D.L. Moody*. Old Tappan, NJ: Fleming H. Revell Co., 1900.

Pollock, J.C. *Moody*. New York: Macmillan Publishing Co., 1963.

THE BOOTHS

Beardsley, Frank G. *Heralds of Salvation*. New York: American Tract Society, 1939.

Begbie, Harold. *The Life of General William Booth*. New York: Macmillan Publishing Co., 1920.

Booth-Tucker, F.deL. *The Life of Catherine Booth*. Old Tappan, NJ: Fleming H. Revell Co., 1892.

Collier, Richard. *The General Next to God*. Cleveland: Collins-World, 1976.

Nelson, William. *General William Booth*. New York: Doran and Company, 1929.

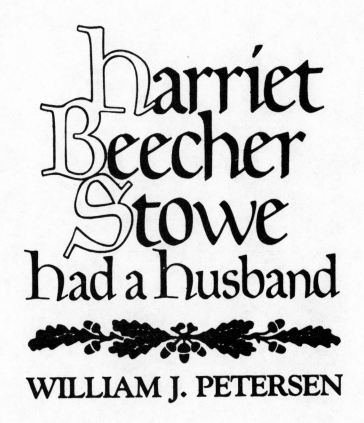

harriet Beecher Stowe had a husband

WILLIAM J. PETERSEN

First printing, May 1983
Library of Congress Catalog Card Number 82-74280
ISBN 0-8423-1329-X
Printed in the United States of America

CONTENTS

At the beginning
of our marriage,
some very wise person
told me that
when two people agree
on everything,
one of them
is unnecessary . . . .
Happy marriages
are never accidental.
They are the result
of good hard work.

RUTH BELL GRAHAM

INTRODUCTION

What do all marriages have in common?

Harriet Beecher and Calvin Stowe, John and Idelette Calvin, Billy and Ruth Graham, Adoniram and Ann Judson, William and Dorothy Carey—all five of these marriages had at least one thing in common, though it may seem that was about all they had!

At least one thing can be said of all of them: All these marriages—like all marriages everywhere—involve two people.

Not very profound, is it?

And yet, it's important to realize. No matter how many changes occur in customs and cultures, a marriage always involves two people. Always has, always will.

Now when you have two of almost anything, even if you have two sticks of wood, you're going to see some sparks if you keep rubbing them against each other.

One problem I have with many books about marriage is that they depict marriage without sparks. I suppose you can have a friction-free marriage if both you and your mate are completely flawless, but, of course, one of the marriage partners usually falls short of that high standard.

Usually it's your mate. Seldom is it you.

Many biographies of great Christian leaders do not give much space to their marriages. It is as if marriage relationships were somehow beneath them. Supposedly, these Christian giants had more important things to do than to work at a marriage.

Yet it is in marriage that the real character of the individual is most clearly seen. It is the testing ground for true spirituality.

Admittedly, marriage to a celebrity—whether the celebrity is religious or otherwise—puts added strain on the relationship. Just imagine: What would it be like to be married to the brilliant Reformer John Calvin? Or for that matter, how many men could handle being known as Mister Harriet Beecher Stowe?

If you didn't feel a call to the mission field, how would you react if asked to join your husband as a pioneer missionary? Dorothy Carey went with her husband, but she fought the idea. Ann Judson, on the other hand, shared her husband's call, but struggled with loneliness. She could handle big crises better than daily problems.

How would you feel if you had to stay home

with five little children, while your husband, Dr. Billy Graham, was holding evangelistic crusades around the world? For that matter, how does a creative, intelligent woman like Ruth Graham adjust to all the demands of her life and her marriage?

Well, you say, these are special people.

I think that, as you read this book, you will discover that their marriages are made out of the same stuff that composes your marriage. The marital problems they face are problems you face as well. And some of these folk, you will soon discover, didn't do as good a job with their marriage as you are doing with yours. What happened, for instance, to the marriage of William and Dorothy Carey? Could anything have been done to prevent the tragic outcome?

In this book I am not emphasizing the notable spiritual accomplishments of these men and women of God. Others have written in detail about how each one carved his or her niche in Christian history. I hope this book will encourage you to get to know these people better by reading a full-length biography.

But for the present, just consider some ordinary marriages (complete with ordinary conflicts, adjustments, sorrows, and successes) of some extraordinary Christians.

William J. Petersen

Meet John and Idelette Calvin

You know about John Calvin, but you've probably never heard of his wife, Idelette.

Although Theologian John Calvin was the "brains" behind the Protestant Reformation in Switzerland and France, he had a few things to learn about marriage and about raising children.

Frankly, he disliked people problems, and marriage inevitably brought problems. But it also brought him some delightful benefits.

The John Calvin you know about may seem stern and bullheaded. But there's another John Calvin, the husband that Idelette knew.

What was it that softened this brilliant thinker?

How well did the marriage between John of the Reformed Church and Idelette the Anabaptist succeed?

Bookish, reticent, determined, and quick-tempered, John Calvin was still a bachelor at thirty-one. But he thought it was time to change the situation.

His encyclopedic mind was like a file of three-by-five cards. Anything he catalogued in it would be preserved forever. He envisioned himself as a scholar and author. Intellectual problems could be readily solved; people problems were an intrusion into his goal-oriented life.

In 1540 he was in Germany—this Frenchman who became best known for his Reformation ministry in Switzerland. That posed some problems in seeking a wife. He had strong views about predestination, but he was no fatalist about marriage. The right woman wouldn't appear on his doorstep; he would have to go out and find her.

He knew what he wanted, and he told his associates (who were even more interested in finding him a wife than he was) what those requirements were: "Always keep in mind what I seek to find in her, for I am none of those insane lovers who embrace also the vices of those with whom they are in love, where they are smitten at first sight with a fine figure. This only is the beauty that allures me: if she is chaste, if not too fussy or fastidious, if economical, if patient, if there is hope that she will be interested about my health."

The search committee worked for a year and a half. Their first recommended candidate was a wealthy German woman in Strasbourg. Her brother, an ardent supporter of Calvin's teachings, conducted a vigorous campaign. Since John Calvin desired to live the life of a scholar, he said, it would be helpful to have a wealthy wife underwriting his labors. You can't live on the royalties from the sales of theological books.

It made sense to Calvin's aides, but not to Calvin. The first problem was that she spoke no French. "A minor problem," said the searchers, who returned to the woman to talk her into trying to learn French. She wasn't very excited about the idea, but if it was the only way for her to marry John Calvin, she would consent to try.

John saw another problem. He described it to his friend William Farel. "You understand, William, that she would bring with her a large dowry, and this could be embarrassing to a poor minister like myself. I feel, too, that she might become dissatisfied with her humbler station in life." He could imagine her looking back to the "good old days" of prosperity and excitement.

Farel wrote back that he had a woman in his congregation who spoke French and who would make a suitable wife for Calvin. She was in her mid-forties, about fifteen years older than Calvin, and was a devout Protestant. She had never been married and Farel hoped that Calvin wouldn't hold that against her.

Apparently Calvin did; he never pursued the matter.

The third choice came from the search committee and apparently interested Calvin. She didn't have any money, so he wouldn't be accused of marrying her for her dowry. He had never met her, for she lived in another city, but her reputation seemed to match Calvin's requirements for a wife. His brother Antoine told him, "Indeed, she is mightily commended by those who are acquainted with her." She sounded good to Calvin, and being the logical man that he was, he was sure that if she met his list of qualifications, she must be the right mate for him. He wrote Farel to get ready for a wedding on the tenth of March, and he dispatched Antoine to bring her to meet him.

It's hard to say what went wrong. Calvin's writings don't disclose any great faults in the woman. And yet the more that John Calvin knew the woman, the more he disliked her. He would have given the word to cross her off the list, but a problem developed. The problem was that the intended bride had now fallen madly in love with John. What was intended to have been a very nonemotional arrangement was now laden with intense feeling.

When he had written to Farel earlier, Calvin had told him, "I make myself look very foolish if it should so happen that my hope fall through again." But it did fall through again. March 10 came and went, and John Calvin was still a bachelor. And the theologian who disliked people problems was ensnared by one.

The intended bride was not only trying to "overwhelm me altogether with her kindness" as Calvin put it, she was also pressing for marriage. Calvin was as determined not to marry her as she was resolved to be his bride. He wouldn't marry her "even if the Lord had altogether demented me," Calvin said, and he prayed, "Most earnestly do I desire to be delivered out of this difficulty."

The job of "delivering him out of the difficulty" was delegated to brother Antoine, who had arranged the meeting in the first place. John couldn't do it by himself.

With three disappointments, John Calvin wasn't sure whether he should put himself into a vulnerable position again. Maybe God wanted him to stay single. He wrote, "I have not yet found a wife and frequently hesitate as to whether I ought any more to seek one." At this point, the search committee seems to have disbanded, whether because of John's discouragement or its own inability to find additional candidates.

Then John remembered a widow in the small congregation which he pastored. With his encyclopedic mind why hadn't he recalled her before? Idelette de Bure Stordeur was his age, thirty-one, and from his station in life. She had cared lovingly for a sick husband, who had died in the plague a few months earlier.

John had converted both of them to the Reformed faith only a year before. She was an intelligent woman who spoke her mind, yet at the same time she had been very supportive of her husband. Besides, she was attractive. For John Calvin that was frosting on the cake.

In less than a month, he had written once again to William Farel to come and officiate at a wedding; within two months John and Idelette were married.

Like Luther, John Calvin can easily be caricatured, but such characterizations are seldom accurate. He was stubborn, quick-tempered, and bookish, but he was also friendly, conciliatory, and kind. You always knew where you stood with John Calvin. A man of iron self-discipline and definite principles, he was still more willing than Luther to work with other Protestants whose views were a shade different from his own.

Born in 1509 in the old cathedral city of Noyon, sixty miles from Paris, he was the son of Gerard Calvin, who worked as business manager and part-time attorney for the Catholic church. John's mother died when he was three; all he could remember was what he had been told about her. There was a stepmother but John didn't like to talk about her.

John's father, a shrewd man, was determined

to get his son the best education his influence could finagle. First, he got John, while still only a boy, appointed to the church office. Technically, it was illegal, but after all, the Archbishop of Rheims received his office at five and the Bishop of Mainz when he had just turned four, so it wasn't too hard for Gerard Calvin to get his son a minor chaplaincy appointment at the age of twelve, especially since the authorities knew that John would be training for the priesthood.

Two years later, at age fourteen, still receiving an honorarium as chaplain, young John went to Paris to attend college. He spent three years in a liberal arts college and one in a school of theology which was noted for its whippings, lice, and rotten eggs. Calvin survived and at age eighteen received a master's degree.

It was 1527, and Luther's writings were infiltrating the corners of France. Jacques LeFevre, a Parisian, had just been evicted from the Sorbonne for his Protestant-sounding books; Calvin's cousin Olivetan had embraced the new teachings. Young John Calvin, however, was not easily swayed.

Then his father got in trouble with the Archbishop. Accusing him of mishandling an estate, the Archbishop demanded that the elder Calvin open his books and reveal the financial records. Stubbornly, Gerard Calvin refused. As a result, he lost his job. Angrily, he wrote his son in Paris, urging him to transfer from theology to law. No longer did he want his son to be studying for the Catholic ministry. Obediently, John did what his father had bidden him to do.

Three years later, however, when his father died, John switched again. Now he had decided to become a classical scholar. Within a year he had published a learned commentary on the Roman philosopher Seneca, written properly in polished Latin.

Nobody bought it, though people said nice things about it. Calvin tried to promote its sales himself, but commercially it was a flop.

It was a blow to the up-and-coming scholar. Previously he had been successful in all his academic pursuits, but as he looked at the interests in his life, all he saw was confusion. He didn't know where to turn. Though he was still defending it, he was becoming increasingly disillusioned with the Roman Catholic church; the legal profession did not excite him; and his attempt in classical scholarship had fizzled.

Calvin didn't know what was going on, yet God did. Calvin later wrote: "God by a sudden conversion subdued my heart." It probably happened in 1533, when John was twenty-four years old, and it was preceded by a string of turbulent events.

A close friend had been made rector of the University of Paris and as part of his responsibility was called upon to make the annual All-Saints Day address. Having received his training in medicine, the rector felt a bit insecure as he prepared his address for the older and more distinguished professors of philosophy and law at the Sorbonne.

In recent months the rector had become quite evangelical in his thinking, and so he had some strong things to say to the Sorbonne. Yet he needed the assistance of a scholar, someone who could support his arguments by the proper classical quotations and references to the church fathers. His friend John Calvin, though not yet convinced about the rector's Protestant leanings, would be glad to help him.

The speech was effective, perhaps too effective. The rector was run out of town, and John Calvin— when word got around that he had helped prepare the speech—became a hunted man as well. As the police were coming to John's apartment, he escaped through a back window on a rope made out of bedclothes. Seeking refuge, he found the home of a former classmate; probably at this time he had his conversion experience.

Calvin told it this way: "Whenever I descended into my soul or raised my mind up to Thee, extreme terror seized me, such terror as no expectations or satisfactions could cure. And the more closely I examined myself, the sharper the stings with which my conscience was pricked, so that the only solace left to me was to delude myself by trying to forget it all. . . . At last I saw in what a pigsty of error I had wallowed, and how polluted and impure I had become. With great fear and tremblings, I could do no other than at once to betake myself to Thy way."

Since his native France was no longer safe for him, he escaped across the border to Basel, Switzerland, where he wrote the first edition of his most famous work, *The Institutes of the Christian Religion*. He completed it when he was twenty-six years old, within a year or two of his conversion.

Finally Calvin had found his career, or so he thought. He would be a Protestant scholar-theologian. As he wrote later, "The summit of my wishes was the enjoyment of literary ease, with something of a free and honorable station." Pictures of Calvin at this period depict a rather dapper young man with a well-tended curly forked beard and a large ring on his left hand. Holding embroidered gloves, he appears the image of a well-bred Frenchman with a concern for his appearance.

In 1534 he had written, "I have learned from experience that we cannot see very far before us." He had already changed career goals four times in the previous eight years. In 1536 he would face another change.

Traveling through Geneva, Switzerland, he was halted by William Farel, a fiery Genevan cleric, who asked him to stay and assist in the reformation of the church there. Calvin knew better. Geneva had a bad reputation. Reforming it would be akin to reforming Sodom and Gomorrah. So Calvin told Farel that he was approaching the wrong man. Calvin was too shy to do what Farel was asking. He was a behind-the-scenes man, a scholar, not a fiery evangelist. His home was a library, not a pulpit.

Farel wouldn't take no for an answer. He responded: "You're using your studies as an excuse; you're being selfish and self-willed. If you don't stay with me in Geneva, God will curse you, for you will be seeking your own honor instead of Christ's."

Believe it or not, that began a lifelong friendship. Calvin stayed. He explained: "I felt as if God from heaven had laid his mighty hand upon me to stop me in my tracks."

In one of his commentaries Calvin described the scribe of Matthew 8:19, probably describing himself as well: "He wants to fight in the shade and at ease, untroubled by sweat or dust, and beyond the reach of weapons of war." Farel put Calvin on the front lines.

And it was a battle, especially for someone like John Calvin, whose headaches and stomach upsets flared up in times of stress. The city council referred to him coldly as "that Frenchman," and most of the town boycotted his daily lectures on Paul's Epistles.

When the council began referring to him by a name, he was called the Protestant Pope. John's temper flared. In the middle of a sermon he called the city fathers a "council of the devil," and that didn't help matters. Later he confessed, "I have been too hasty; I have tried to do too much too quickly."

Shortly after Easter 1538, Farel and Calvin were given three days to get out of town. A contemporary reporter said that it was a special miracle that they were able to get out before blood was shed.

Calvin resolved never again to return to Geneva and never again to get mixed up in church affairs. People problems caused his headaches. From now on, he would be engaged in scholarly pursuits. But hardly had he unpacked his books in Basel when he received an urgent letter from a pastor in Strasbourg, Germany, urging him to come and help with a church of French refugees. Naturally, Calvin turned him down. "I shall retire in Basel," he wrote. He was not quite twenty-nine years old.

But the Strasbourg leader Martin Bucer came back with a stronger letter. It pulled no punches. "God will know how to find the rebellious servant, as he found Jonah, if you try to run away from Him." It almost sounded like William Farel talking, and Calvin didn't know how to turn down orders like that. Hurriedly, he headed for Strasbourg.

The congregation of French refugees, though growing, was small, and so Calvin took on additional responsibilities as professor of theology at the newly formed University of Strasbourg. Neither job provided him with much income.

At first Calvin stayed in Bucer's home. Bucer was not only a happily married man, but he considered it one of his callings in life to get his assistants married as well. Once after Calvin had lost his temper, Bucer suggested, "John, you ought to have a wife." Calvin wasn't quite sure how the two things were related, but he told Bucer that he would consider it.

Because Calvin needed money to live on, he sold part of his library and rented a large house which he turned into a dormitory for students. "My poverty is so great that at present I do not even have a sou," he wrote Farel. But he soon discovered that running a boarding house was full of people problems, which aggravated his headaches and caused stomach upsets as well. So he hired a cook-housekeeper with a sharp tongue and slovenly housekeeping habits. Though he tried to stay as far away from her as possible, there was no room in the house that wasn't pierced when she began screaming at a tenant. Calvin was trying to revise the second edition of the *Institutes* at the time and didn't know what to do with her. On the other hand, he didn't know what he would do without her either. Maybe if he had a wife, she would know how to handle people problems like that.

Idelette de Bure had already lived a full life at thirty-one. A native of Gelderland, Holland, she had married Jean Stordeur of Liege when she was sixteen or seventeen. Two children were born—Jacques and Judith—and then Idelette and Jean were converted by Anabaptist missionaries.

Conversion to Anabaptist beliefs meant persecution. Idelette wasn't concerned for herself, but she was concerned for her children. If she and her husband were martyred, what would become of Jacques and Judith?

In the Low Countries of Belgium and the Netherlands, thousands of Anabaptists were slain; some historians have put the figure as high as 30,000. Menno Simons wrote about it: "Some they have hanged, some they have punished with inhuman tyranny and afterward garroted them with cords, tied to a post. Some they have roasted and burned alive. Some, holding their own entrails in their hands, have powerfully confessed the Word of God still. Some they beheaded and gave as food to the fowls of the air. Some they have consigned to the fish. They have torn down the houses of some. Some have they thrust into muddy bogs. . . . They must take to their heels and flee away with their wives and little children, from one city to another—hated by all men, abused, slandered, mocked, defamed, trampled upon."

Little wonder that Idelette was concerned for her children.

Throughout Europe, Strasbourg was known as a free city, a refuge from religious oppression. Some of the earlier Anabaptists had believed that Strasbourg was the city where God would set up a new Jerusalem. Probably Idelette and Jean came simply to find a place where they could raise their children in peace. They followed other refugees to the church in which John Calvin ministered. His preaching was so biblical, so clear, so logical, so convincing that soon they were convinced, along with many other Anabaptist refugees, that Calvin's views of Scripture made sense.

In the small congregation where new members were catechized, Calvin must have taken some special interest in the spiritual progress of these new converts, the Stordeurs. And he must have sorrowed when he heard that Jean Stordeur had become ill.

God had preserved Jean Stordeur from the flames of martyrdom in Holland, but not the pestilential plague in Strasbourg. And there, not much more than a year after they had arrived, he was buried. No doubt it was one of the first funerals that Calvin conducted in Strasbourg. He couldn't have helped noticing the attractive, gentle woman dressed in black who looked too young to be the mother of the twelve-year-old son and the six-year-old daughter who walked behind.

By this time Calvin had become a bit discouraged in his quest for a wife. However, he was still in the market for one. After all, three of the men that he respected most—Farel, Bucer, and even Luther's friend Philip Melanchthon—had urged him to consider it. Often the major moves of Calvin's life had been because of such urgings of friends and family. His father had told him to change from theology to law. Farel had stopped him in Geneva. Bucer had called him to come to Strasbourg; and now Bucer, Farel, and Melanchthon had all ganged up on him to get married.

Prior to Strasbourg, Calvin hadn't had many models of marriage. He knew little about the relationship of his mother and father. In Geneva his closest friend had been Farel, a fifty-year-old bachelor. So it wasn't until he had arrived in the home of Bucer in Strasbourg that he saw a Christian marriage. A deep love and warm camaraderie were evident. Elizabeth Bucer was a good mother, a hospitable homemaker, and her husband's best critic. Bucer regarded the last point as the most important. But visitors to the home, as John Calvin had been, noticed most of all the way Elizabeth Bucer opened her home to refugees. One visitor wrote: "For seventeen days after my arrival, I was entertained in Bucer's home. It is like a hostel, receiving refugees for the cause of Christ. In his family during the entire time I saw not the least occasion of offense but only ground for edification. I never left the table without having learned something."

In Strasbourg the senior minister was Matthew

Zell, whose wife was the remarkably outspoken Katherine Zell. Her husband, who had been a priest, was roundly criticized for marrying her. He refused to reply to the criticisms, but she wasn't hesitant. She penned a biblical defense of clerical marriage, as well as a defense for herself, a woman writing to instruct theologians: "I do not pretend to be John the Baptist rebuking the Pharisees," she wrote. "I aspire only to be Balaam's ass, castigating his master."

Like Elizabeth Bucer, she housed refugees in her parsonage. At one time eighty found a haven there.

Once she wrote a letter to Luther urging him to reach an agreement with other Protestant leaders, and once when John Calvin had a temper tantrum in their home, it was Katherine who mollified him. The marriages of the Bucers and the Zells must have influenced John.

Just at the time when Calvin was beginning to think of marriage, he met Philip Melanchthon, Luther's associate. They became good friends. Melanchthon, who had now been married for nineteen years, was one of those who encouraged Calvin to follow suit, no doubt sharing his personal testimony with him. Mrs. Melanchthon, who had a rollicking sense of humor, took good care of Philip both physically and emotionally. Melanchthon's one complaint was, "She always thinks that I am dying of hunger unless I am stuffed like a sausage."

Thus, when Calvin began noticing Idelette, the attractive widow in his congregation, his concept of marriage had evolved a bit from the mechanical checklist of requirements with which he had begun his search.

Farel, who had been alerted at least twice before to an impending marriage, found that this was no false alarm. Idelette and John were both ready for marriage. Farel took delight in performing the ceremony.

The biggest problem in their marriage soon became evident; it was a health problem. Both of them had frequent bouts with illness. Hardly had Farel pronounced them man and wife when both of them became ill. A week or two later, Calvin sent a thank-you note to Farel from his bed: "As if it had been so ordered, that our wedlock might not be overjoyous, the Lord thus thwarted our joy by moderating it."

They had barely recovered from that illness when another string of events confined them both to bed again. It started when Calvin's tart-tongued housekeeper insulted his brother Antoine, who was staying at the Calvin dormitory. Antoine walked out, vowing never to return as long as the housekeeper remained. To Calvin, it was the last straw, and his temper almost erupted against the surly housekeeper. Knowing that the volcano was soon to blow, the housekeeper quit after preparing the evening meal. Trying to control himself, Calvin was still seething. "I am wont," he explained later, "when heated to anger, or stirred by some greater anxiety than usual, to eat to excess . . . which so happened to me at that time." The next morning he had a severe digestive attack but carried on his preaching and teaching duties anyway. By evening he was running a fever and he fainted from his weakened condition. That put him in bed, after which Idelette got the bug. "While I was still suffering under the weakness, my wife took a fever. The last eight days she has been so exhausted . . . that she can with difficulty sit up in bed."

Though Calvin did not share as much of his home life in his writings as Luther did, you get from Calvin's letters a glimpse of Idelette as one who cared deeply for John's well-being and for her children. At times she accompanied him on trips; sometimes John mentions their entertaining guests in their home. Calvin's biographers refer to her as "a woman of some force and individuality," and John himself describes her as "the faithful helper of my ministry" and "the best companion of my life."

During the first ten months of their marriage, however, companionship wasn't the hallmark of their relationship. It's true, of course, that they were companions in sickness during the first two months after their wedding. Then Calvin was urged to attend an important theological gathering in Worms, Germany. He wasn't eager to go, for several reasons, primarily because he didn't want to leave Idelette and because he was still weakened by his recent illnesses. But he felt he had no choice in the matter.

About a year earlier, Emperor Charles, ruler of the Holy Roman Empire, had summoned the leading Catholic and Protestant scholars to a summit conference. The emperor wasn't really concerned about theological matters; what bothered him was the fact that the Turks were menacing his empire, and with the Catholics and Protestants squabbling among themselves, he couldn't form a united military front against the Turks. Therefore, he proposed a unity conference.

Most of those attending were German theologians, and Calvin, a thirty-one-year-old Frenchman, was flattered to be asked. But he remarked candidly, "I expect little from it." His expectations were accurate. Prior to his marriage two of these meetings had already been held. Neither had accomplished much. The third was scheduled for November 1, 1540, in Worms.

Calvin soon had second thoughts about his decision to attend. The duke who was to chair the conference didn't show up until December 1, and then it took six weeks of arguing to agree on the agenda and the form of the debate. The debate itself lasted only a week. During all this time, Idelette the newlywed was home in Strasbourg, taking care of John's boarding house and her two children.

John got back home late in January 1541. After one month back home, he headed to eastern Germany for the last of the series of conferences. "I am dragged most unwillingly to Ratisbon," Calvin wrote. But he went.

Several hundred miles from home, he received news that a plague was ravaging Strasbourg. Calvin was worried. "Day and night my wife has been constantly in my thoughts," he wrote. The previous plague had taken Idelette's first husband; this plague could easily take Idelette, who was already weakened by recent illness. He wrote advising her to leave town. But Idelette had taken matters into her own hands and had accompanied her children to her brother's home.

Idelette stayed out of town for several weeks, but not as long as her husband stayed at the emperor's theological conference. The gathering which had begun in March was still going strong four months later in June when John Calvin walked out and headed home to Idelette. By the end of June, Calvin had been married forty-five weeks and had been away from home for thirty-two of them.

But more than Idelette was on his mind. It had been three years since he had been kicked out of Geneva, and for the past two years he had been getting letters begging him to return. At first the letters had come from private citizens: "Everyone sighs for you," or "Come, come that we may rejoice in God our Redeemer." To put it mildly,

John was not eager to return. "I would rather face death a hundred times" than return to Geneva, he wrote. When a pastor in Lausanne urged him to return to Geneva and mentioned that the climate would be good for his health, Calvin retorted by calling Geneva a torture chamber and asking how the good pastor could have an interest in his health and still urge him to return.

For Calvin, Geneva was the last place in the world in which he wanted to live. No doubt his concern for Idelette contributed to his strong feelings. She had known as much suffering as he had, probably more. If a second sojourn in Geneva would be anything like his first two years there, the problems would be endless. Strasbourg was a haven, even though it had its problems, too. But problems in Strasbourg could be faced and forgotten. Geneva's problems were perpetual. Looking at himself and his own talents, he realized that God had given him the gifts of a scholar, not the cast-iron stomach of a barroom brawler. It made no sense to him to consider returning to Geneva.

But the letters from Geneva became more insistent and sounded more desperate. Now they were coming from the city council itself. And even William Farel was begging him to return. He hated it when Farel turned his guns on him.

Calvin roared back: "You have deeply distressed me with your thundering and lightning. Why do you make me look so bad and feel so guilty? Do you want me to renounce your friendship? . . . If I had a free choice, I would prefer doing anything else in the world."

Two months after his marriage, an official Geneva delegation came to Strasbourg, just after Calvin had gotten off his sickbed and gone to the conference in Worms. Undeterred, the delegation continued to Worms to deliver their message.

Calvin read Geneva's official invitation and then burst into tears. "The very thought of Geneva is agony to me."

Sometime early in 1541, his decision was made. "It is difficult to overcome my soul and control it, but I know that I am not my own master. I offer my heart to the Lord in sacrifice."

Then in the month of September, Calvin headed to Geneva. Some scholars feel that Calvin may have hoped that he could settle some matters there in a few weeks and then return home. But most feel that he was testing the sincerity of the council's invitation. At any rate, Idelette stayed behind in Strasbourg until John found out whether or not Geneva would be safe for her.

The city council did their best to accommodate the Calvins. They were promised a handsome salary (some of which was to be used to entertain prominent guests). The council also purchased a house for the Calvins and guaranteed their safety. Furthermore, they sent an escort to bring Idelette and all the family furniture to Geneva. John concluded that the "natives" might be friendly after all.

During their first summer back in Geneva, Idelette bore a son prematurely. Little Jacques died when only two weeks old. For both John and Idelette, it was a severe emotional blow. John wrote a fellow pastor, "The Lord has certainly inflicted a bitter wound in the death of our infant son. But He is Himself a father and knows what is good for His children."

Three years later, a daughter died at birth, and two years after that, when both John and Idelette were thirty-nine, a third child was born prematurely and died. Idelette's physical problems worsened. Coughing spells dragged her down.

Idelette, of course, had two children by her first husband. Her son stayed in Strasbourg to complete his studies. Her daughter, who grew more rebellious in teenage years, became part of the Calvin home in Geneva.

Their Geneva home was at Number 11, Rue de Chanoines. The city council had loaned them furniture to help fill it. It had three bedrooms upstairs, and a living room, study, and kitchen downstairs. At the top of the short street was a water fountain where Idelette could wash clothes and draw water for the family.

The home wasn't large, but there was always someone staying in the third bedroom. For much of the time it was John's brother Antoine and his wife, and this was a help to Idelette. Behind the house was a garden, sloping down to the city walls. Herbs and flowers scented the air, and John enjoyed showing his guests where Idelette grew vegetables.

John's schedule was exhausting. He preached two Sunday sermons, conducted weekday services every other week, and on Tuesdays, Thursdays, and Saturdays gave theological lectures. Thursday was also his day to conduct elders' meetings, and on Friday he had a Bible study with the other preachers in town.

When Idelette was well enough, she accompanied her husband in visiting the sick and those in prison. She had a deep concern for those who were suffering. In John's spare time he wrote letters. In fact, he wrote so many of them that his home became a branch post office.

Amazingly, John was able to keep to this schedule even though his health was poor. Migraine headaches, stomach ulcers, asthma, and pleurisy were among his problems. The feeling that he was being constantly thrust into people problems, which he disliked, aggravated his physical maladies.

A timid man, he is described by John T. McNeill as "one of those scholarly and highly sensitive persons whose talents mark them for prominent leadership, and who shrink from but dare not shirk the duties involved. Such persons may become assertive even in overcoming an inclination to retirement."

"God thrust me into the game," Calvin once said, and Calvin played games seriously. At home he liked to play games when time permitted. His favorites were quoits (a sort of ring-toss) and bowls (indoor bowling), as well as a key-toss game. John Knox reported that, when he called at Calvin's home one Sunday afternoon, he found him playing bowls.

But the game into which God had thrust him in Geneva wasn't that much fun despite the early promises of the city council. Calvin had as many enemies in the city as he had friends, and they made life miserable. They called their dogs "Calvin." What angered John more, however, was to hear Idelette insulted; because of her Anabaptist background, Calvin's enemies called her first marriage an illegitimate one.

Despite her ill health, Idelette did a good job of keeping John on an even keel. Friends noticed that John seemed better able to control his temper since he had become married, in spite of the continuing provocations.

Idelette's health went steadily downhill. In August 1548 Calvin wrote, "She is so overpowered with her sickness that she can scarcely support herself." It was probably tuberculosis.

She never wanted her health problems to burden her husband. He had enough problems in Geneva without her adding her physical problems to them. But in 1549 Idelette lay dying. She was only forty and had been married to John for only nine years. As she neared death, she asked John to care for her two children. She hated to add to his load. "I have committed them to the Lord," she told him in short gasping phrases, "but I want you to promise that you will not neglect them." He promised.

Three days later, Idelette was still lingering, but John knew that death was only a few hours away. Her last words were "O glorious resurrection." Then when she was unable to speak any longer, John spoke to her about Christ's love, about eternal life, and about the blessings of their nine years together. An hour later, Idelette was gone.

Calvin was grief-stricken. A week later he wrote to a pastor friend: "Truly mine is no ordinary grief." And to his friend Farel he wrote, "I do what I can to keep myself from being overwhelmed with grief. My friends also leave nothing undone that may bring relief to my mental suffering. . . . May the Lord Jesus . . . support me under this heavy affliction, which would certainly have overcome me had not He who raises up the prostrate, strengthens the weak and refreshes the weary, stretched forth His hand from heaven to me."

In a few weeks one of his friends wrote back: "I know, friend, your innate tenderness. So I write to you a letter of congratulations rather than one of condolence. . . . With admiration, I experience the power of God's Spirit who works in you and shows Himself in you as Comforter. How well do I know how deeply this had wounded you, for nothing more difficult could have happened to you. How you must feel, you whom the grief of others moves so deeply."

Calvin, though only forty, never remarried. A year after Idelette's death, he spoke of her uniqueness and pledged that he intended henceforth "to lead a solitary life."

He lived fifteen more years, shaping the city of Geneva, revising once again his masterpiece, *Institutes of the Christian Religion*, and preaching verse by verse through thirty books of the Bible.

His public life seemed busier than ever, but his home life remained solitary.

It is unfortunate that more is not known of the marriage of John and Idelette. The marriage was short—only nine years—and was hampered by bouts with poor health. But it was a good marriage for both of them.

For Idelette, it brought a meaning and purpose to life, and it provided a father for her children.

And for John, who was somewhat of a hypochondriac in addition to suffering from real ills, God provided someone to care for and to love. John had been looking for someone who could care for him, and God sent him someone to care for.

What marriage did for John was to evoke from

him a more tender side than the world normally saw. John is perhaps best known for his theological emphasis on God the Father as Sovereign of the world. Through Idelette, John came to appreciate the ministry of the Holy Spirit as Comforter in the home.

CHAPTER
TWO

Meet William and Dorothy Carey

When William Carey sailed to India in 1793, he launched the modern missionary movement. David Livingstone, Hudson Taylor, Adoniram Judson, and thousands of others followed his example, taking the gospel message to those who had never heard it.

William Carey was the pioneer among missionary pioneers and the Bible translator *par excellence.* So you will certainly want to meet William Carey. He was a most remarkable man.

But don't forget Dorothy Carey. She may be over in the corner or she may be trying to manage the children or she may have gone home early.

I may as well tell you openly: Dorothy had emotional problems.

William and Dorothy lived in a day before psychologists and counselors, so they didn't have the benefit of scores of books that may have given them some understanding.

Would you like to play the role of amateur psychologist for Dorothy? What counsel would you give to help William and Dorothy understand themselves and each other? Could anything have been done to help Dorothy be a productive servant of the Lord?

In the process of answering these questions, you might find some clues that will help you preserve the mental health of your own marriage.

What drove Dorothy Carey insane?

If it is proper to call William Carey the father of the modern missionary movement, what would you call Dorothy?

If William was somewhat of a self-made man, was Dorothy a self-destructive woman? Or was it something in the mix of the two that made them what they came to be?

As you can guess, the marriage of William and Dorothy Carey was not exactly idyllic.

For more than forty years, William Carey pioneered—he would say *plodded*—as a missionary to India. Dorothy lasted fourteen years, reluctantly and pitifully.

The story of William Carey, the humble shoemaker who became a brilliant missionary linguist, is one of those spiritual Horatio Alger stories of how God plucked an unlikely candidate to be the leader of a multitude. But what about poor Dorothy?

Let's begin with William:

Hometown: Paulerspury, an obscure village about eighty miles north of London.

Year of Birth: 1761, fifteen years before the American Revolution.

Father: Edmund Carey, a journeyman weaver who worked with woolen cloth on a loom in their small cottage.

Family Income: About ten shillings a week.

Family Members: Sharing the cottage with Edmund and his rather large loom were his wife, Elizabeth, their five children, and Edmund's mother. William was the oldest child.

Not content with being a journeyman weaver, Edmund was named parish clerk and schoolmaster when William was six. In communities like Paulerspury which happened to have a charity school, poor children between seven and twelve years of age could learn the three R's and religion up to the level of the schoolmaster's understanding—which often wasn't very high.

Thus, William not only had the privilege of a

few years of education, but also had access to books because of his father's position, and he became an insatiable reader. Books like *Robinson Crusoe* and *Gulliver's Travels* telling of imagined travels around the world had been published fifty years earlier. William read them and dreamed.

At the age of twelve, when his schooling ended, he began to work in the fields. But two years later a skin rash developed whenever he worked in the hot sun, so he had to shift careers. A shoemaker took him on as an apprentice.

William slid to the level of the boys that hung around the blacksmith's shop. He later spoke of his addiction to "swearing, lying and unchaste conversation," and of being led "into the depths of that gross conduct which prevails among the lower classes in the most neglected villages." He also liked a good argument. He called his teenage years "restless." "I wanted something," he wrote later, "but had no idea that nothing but an entire change of heart could do me good."

Then one Christmas, while making deliveries for his employer, he was given a couple of tips. Among the tips was a counterfeit shilling. He decided to tell his boss that it had been given as payment for some shoes. Thus, his boss had the counterfeit coin and William kept as his tip a genuine shilling from an actual payment. When his boss somehow discovered the deceitful exchange, William was both shamed and frightened.

The lie had been bad enough, but British law was extremely strict about thievery. The theft of more than a shilling was grand larceny and that was a capital offense.

In his shame, Carey refused to go to church for a while. But that didn't stop him from arguing about religion with a fellow apprentice who went to a Dissenter church. Eventually, Carey agreed to attend church with his friend. Hearing a sermon on Hebrews 13:13: "Let us therefore go out unto him without the camp, bearing his reproach," Carey, now seventeen, made his commitment to Christ. At the same time, he left the established Anglican church where his father and mother worshiped, and joined the Dissenters' Congregational church.

When Carey's employer died, another cobbler hired him as an apprentice, and within two years Carey married his new employer's sister-in-law, Dorothy (Dolly) Plackett. Nothing is known of their courtship.

Carey was nineteen; she was twenty-five. He was short and slight, a cobbler's apprentice, making five or six shillings a week. She was illiterate, the daughter of the lay leader of the Congregational church in Piddington which Carey now attended. There was no charity school in Piddington. Even if there had been one, Dorothy wouldn't have been able to attend because, for one thing, her parents were Dissenters and for another, she was a girl. So at the time of her marriage to William, she signed the church's register with a "large, wobbly cross."

They were extremely poor, but they didn't seem to notice. Within a year they had another mouth to feed, a daughter named Ann. Behind the shanty which they called home, William planted a garden. When he wasn't cobbling or gardening, William was reading or studying Greek. Or preaching. The church at which he preached regularly was eight miles away. He walked both ways. The tiny congregation was so poor that "he did not receive enough for the clothes he wore out in their service."

Once a month he also preached in the Dissenters' church in his home town of Paulerspury, much to the embarrassment of his father, who was serving as a parish clerk of the Anglican church. His sister recalled: "We should rather have wished him to go *from* home, rather than come home to preach."

His sister also recalled his zealousness: "Like Gideon, he seemed for throwing down all the altars of Baal in one night." She also resented a certain self-righteousness in his youthful enthusiasm: "Nothing but my love for my brother would have kept me from showing my resentment."

Yes, that first year of marriage was exciting for William. The birth of a daughter made it exciting for Dorothy, too. But obviously, she couldn't walk with William to the church at which he preached, and with the baby she couldn't attend her parents' church very often either. And of course, she couldn't share in William's study of Greek. It was enough of a struggle for her to learn the English alphabet.

Year two of the marriage was more traumatic than exciting. Daughter Ann died, and Dorothy was crushed by the loss. Then the same disease struck William. With him bedridden, the poverty-stricken family was destitute. Unable to cope with the calamities, Dorothy started to retreat from reality. Everything she loved was being taken away from her, and she was helpless. When William's mother came to visit, she was appalled at the living conditions of the home. William's teenaged brother gave him what he could to help the family. His home town of Paulerspury took up a special offering to enable William and Dorothy to buy a small cottage in a better part of Piddington.

The high fever left William bald at twenty-one. And the daughter's death left Dorothy despondent and fearful. William bought a wig; Dorothy found nothing to cover her emotional hurts.

Economically, the following years weren't much easier. When twenty-two, William officially became a Baptist by being immersed in the River

Nene. The records of John Ryland, who baptized him, say, "This day baptized a poor journeyman shoemaker."

Two months later, when William's master died, the "poor journeyman shoemaker" took over the business. He also took over the care of the master's widow and her four children. Unfortunately, it was not the best of years for business in Great Britain. The country was licking its wounds after its humiliating defeat in America's Revolutionary War. Some customers were cutting back on their orders, others had cancelled their orders completely, and William was faced with many customers refusing to pay for shoes that had previously been ordered.

It was a mercy when William, now twenty-three, got a call from a Baptist church in nearby Moulton. Moulton had been without a pastor for ten years, and the salary was on a par with what William had been getting as a cobbler—about fifteen pounds a year. But at least he wouldn't have to worry about cancelled orders, and now he could do what he enjoyed doing. He never thought he was a good shoemaker anyway.

To supplement his income, he taught school. He didn't do very well at that either, because he couldn't discipline the children. "When I kept school," he said candidly, "the boys kept me." He occasionally had to return to some part-time shoemaking to make ends meet. For William, Dorothy, and their infant son Felix, it continued to be a meager existence. One observer wrote, "He and his family have lived for a great while together without tasting animal food and with but a scanty pittance for other provisions." One of the provisions that Carey spent money on was secondhand books. To him they were more important than meat; Dorothy would rather have had the meat.

After four years of preaching, Carey decided that it was time for him to be ordained. But he was turned down. His preaching was criticized as colorless; he was asked to try again in two years. Nevertheless he continued pastoring the church at Moulton that no one else wanted. In his spare time he learned foreign languages—Greek, Latin, Hebrew, French, Dutch, and Italian—all of which were relatively easy for him. Dorothy, meanwhile, was still struggling with English.

Besides languages, Carey was fascinated with geography. A neighboring pastor who visited Carey when he was cobbling again wrote, "I remember that on going into the room where he employed himself at his business, I saw hanging up against the wall a very large map consisting of several sheets of paper pasted together by himself on which he had drawn with a pen a place for every nation in the known world and had entered into it whatever he met with in reading, relative to its population, religion, etc. These researches, on which his mind was naturally bent, hindered him, of course, from doing much at his business . . .

and he was at this time exposed to great hardships."

Nobody knew the hardships better than Dorothy. The family was growing. Between 1785 and 1790, four children were born, and William wasn't much help in changing diapers. Biographer Mary Drewery writes: "The strain must have been particularly great for Dorothy with her young husband so completely absorbed in his preaching and studying—interests which it would be difficult for an unlettered girl to share. She must have felt at times very much alone. Carey drove himself relentlessly, disciplined himself and used every minute of every day."

Somewhere in the course of the marriage, William apparently taught Dorothy how to read and write, though it doesn't seem as if she used these newly acquired skills any more than necessary.

Dorothy may have been fearful and insecure, but she was also stubborn. She had a mind of her own. And William apparently was so concerned about disciplining his mind that he was not concerned if his children were undisciplined in behavior.

In 1787 Dorothy decided to be baptized by immersion. William had been immersed in 1783 and had been a Baptist minister since 1785. But not until two years later did Dorothy submit to immersion. William must have taken great delight in performing the baptism.

Quite possibly she felt neglected, even abandoned, by her husband. He seemed always to have important things to do. William's parents had the same problem with him; they wondered why they seldom saw him or heard from him despite his living only fifteen miles away. In response to his father's irritation, William spelled out his busy weekly schedule and said, "You will see that you must not expect frequent letters."

As William moved into his world of dreaming the impossible, Dorothy gradually drifted into her dream world, too. William's world was growing; Dorothy's was shrinking. Besides the big homemade map on his wall, Carey enjoyed the stimulation of regular ministers' meetings and the rather radical Philosophical Institute which met in Leicester. Coming from a lower class, Carey supported both the American and the French Revolutions, and as a religious dissenter, he hoped and prayed for a revolution of sorts in England.

From the time of his ordination, Carey had been pushing his fellow ministers for involvement in foreign missions. At first his fellow pastors looked at him as an uneducated young upstart and humored him. Then finally a senior minister put him in his place by calling him a "miserable enthusiast" and by informing him that if God wanted to save the heathen, He was sovereign and would do it in His own way, "without your aid or mine, young man."

Carey went home, looked at the huge map on the wall, read the Great Commission, and decided he would write out his reasons why foreign missionary efforts should be launched. When he presented his reasons, his paper got no farther than his oral pleas. His fellow ministers thought it "was a wild and impracticable scheme that he had got in his mind, and therefore gave him no encouragement."

But he didn't give up. At this point in his life, it would have been easy for him to quit, but he didn't. He may not have been a natural leader, but he was a natural plodder. He may have failed as a cobbler, as a teacher, and even as a husband. But he wasn't going to quit in his burden for a missionary outreach.

Nearly five years later, Carey published his treatise, now a bit more polished, with a forty-one-word title beginning *An Enquiry into the Obligations of Christians. . . .*" It was a masterpiece, chopping all opposing arguments into shreds.

Three weeks after its publication, Carey was invited to speak at the ministers' meeting, and his fellow clergymen knew what he would be talking about. He was thirty-one now and had matured in many ways, but when it came to the ministers' meeting, Carey had a one-track mind. His text was Isaiah 54:2, 3 ("Enlarge the place of thy tent"), and the motto that he hammered home was this: "Expect great things from God; attempt great things for God."

Despite Carey's emotional cry for the establishment of a missionary society, the ministers did not respond. Most of them represented congregations almost as poor as Carey's. Then, as the meeting was about to adjourn, an exasperated William Carey asked the chairman, "Is nothing *again* going to be done?"

That extra shove got the ball rolling. At the next meeting, the Particular Baptist Society for the Propagation of the Gospel among the Heathen—the first British missions society—was officially formed.

Carey thought that Tahiti or Africa would be good places to start, but when a medical doctor, John Thomas, showed up, it made more sense to start with India. Thomas, who had formerly worked with the East India Company in Calcutta, was eager to go back as a missionary, and Carey was eager to go with him.

Carey had waited several years for his fellow ministers, but now things were happening so quickly he was hardly prepared for them. Without question, however, he was more prepared than Dorothy.

Carey was still thirty-one, Dorothy thirty-seven. They had three boys: Felix, eight; William, five; and Peter, three. Lucy, their youngest, had died during the past year while William was preparing the final version of his *Enquiry*. Dorothy couldn't help but resent the ugly map with all the scribbling on it, tacked upon the wall. She couldn't understand why William wouldn't be content to stay where he was. With Lucy's death, she had become depressed again. And now in February 1793, she was five months pregnant, expecting to bear a sixth child before summer. More than ever, she needed security, love, and attention.

But William couldn't stop now. At the January meeting, one of the pastors had said, "There's a gold mine in India, as deep as the center of the earth."

"I'll go down," Carey was reported to have said, "but remember you must hold the ropes."

No, William Carey couldn't stop. He had gone too far for that. So it must have come as a severe jolt to him when Dorothy said bluntly, "I'm not going." He was hoping that she would change her mind before their scheduled sailing date in April.

Dorothy wasn't the only one who couldn't understand William's eagerness to go to India. His church didn't want him to leave either. They had had a hard time finding a pastor before he had come, and they had grown rather fond of him.

Of course, William's father couldn't understand it either. "Is he mad?" he asked, thinking of the lad who twenty years earlier had left farming because he couldn't stand the heat. Now William was heading for India, of all places.

But William was determined to go to India. He wrote his father: "I have many sacrifices to make. I must part with a beloved family and a number of most affectionate friends. Never did I see such sorrow manifested as reigned through our place of worship last Lord's Day. But I have set my hand to the plow."

William knew that he would have to leave his church behind, and he knew he would have to leave his father with the knowledge that he would probably never see him again. But he hoped he would not have to leave his wife behind. Yet he felt he must do what God was calling him to do.

No doubt many were shocked by Dorothy's decision. It was accepted that a wife would blindly follow her husband wherever he would lead. It was unthinkable for her to refuse to go with him.

But consider Dorothy. Here she was "unlettered, unimaginative," as Mary Drewery puts it, and was "expected to venture halfway around the world to a country with a strange people, strange languages, strange climate and customs, with no settled home to go to."

Dorothy needed security. She needed a "settled home." She probably had good reason to question her husband's judgment. They had been married twelve years now, and they had made several moves already, none of which seemed to make life easier for her. They had lived in Hackleton, Piddington, Moulton, and Leicester; William had tried his hand at shoemaking—as an apprentice, as a manager, as a journeyman; he had tried teaching school twice, and had served as pastor of three churches. It would be understandable why Dorothy would not have a deep sense of security in following her husband to India.

Her children must have also concerned her. She had already seen two of them die in her arms; now her husband was asking her to board ship knowing that she was five months pregnant and that she, at thirty-seven, would be having her child before landing in India. There would be scores of men on board, mostly roughhewn sailors, but only one other woman. Yes, Dorothy had plenty to fear.

No doubt, she had also heard that France had just declared war on England, so all British vessels were in danger of attack on the high seas. Voyages under normal conditions were hazardous; in wartime, civilian travel was foolhardy.

William finally accepted Dorothy's decision. The agreement was this: eight-year-old Felix would accompany him to India, but Dorothy and the two younger boys would move back to Piddington where she would share a cottage with her younger sister, Kitty. After a three-year term in India, during which time he would prepare a suitable home for his family, he would return and fetch Dorothy from Piddington.

So in April 1793, Dr. Thomas, his wife, and their daughter, along with William Carey and Felix, set sail for India, down the Thames into the English Channel, then westward along the southern coast of England to the Isle of Wight. And there they stopped. Contrary winds and the hazards of French military action caused the ship's captain to delay sailing any farther.

The delay brought good news and bad news to Carey. The good news was that a delay in departure might give Dorothy a chance to change her mind. The bad news concerned Dr. John Thomas, the medical missionary. Thomas was motivated to sail to India not only by the Great Commission but also by some "great omissions." He had a bad habit of not paying his bills. Consequently, he had a dire need to get out of the country. In Carey's words, Thomas's creditors were hunting him "like a partridge." Thomas was affable enough but always getting deeper in debt.

While Thomas was eagerly trying to book passage on another ship to India, Carey wrote to Dorothy. Word soon came back that his wife had given birth to a fourth son. William responded immediately: "This is pleasant news indeed to me. Surely goodness and mercy follow me all my days, but now I see the goodnesss of God in it." Then he got to the point. "If I had all the world, I would freely give it all to have you and my dear children with me; but the sense of duty is so strong as to overpower all other considerations. I could not turn back without guilt on my soul. . . . You want to know what Mrs. Thomas thinks, and how she likes the voyage. . . . She would rather stay in England than go to India, but thinks it right to go with her husband."

William was surely hoping that Dorothy would take the hint.

His letter continues: "Tell my dear children I love them dearly and pray for them constantly. Felix sends his love. . . . Trust in God. Love to Kitty, brothers, sisters, etc. Be assured I love you most affectionately. Let me know my dear little child's name."

Then William added as a postscript, "My health was never so well. I believe the sea makes Felix and me both as hungry as hunters. Farewell."

The letter, though warm and affectionate, did not budge Dorothy. She was resolute in her decision to stay in Piddington. As Drewery writes, "She must have been a woman of exceptional stubbornness or else Carey must have been more than usually tender and considerate, for, at that period, women were completely subject to the dictates of their husbands."

William joined Dr. Thomas in London, seeking a ship to India. When they finally found a Danish ship that would be departing in five days, William decided he would try one more time to change Dorothy's mind. William, along with son Felix and Dr. Thomas, traveled overnight to get to Piddington at breakfast. Dorothy was overjoyed to see her husband, but she wasn't persuaded by his arguments. Her baby was only a few weeks old. "I had better stay here with Kitty," she said.

Discouraged, they left to visit their mission leaders at the nearby headquarters. Then Dr. Thomas suggested they return to Piddington to try again. Carey said it was useless and besides, "We are losing time." But on this visit to Piddington, Thomas did most of the talking; he told Dorothy that if she didn't come with them, "she would repent it as long as she lived."

Reluctantly, she gave in with the proviso that her sister Kitty be allowed to accompany them. William gladly agreed.

Thanks to the goodness of the ship's captain, the Carey family got the best cabin on the craft even though they were sailing at half price. The voyage was relatively uneventful but it lasted five months, and they didn't stop at any port en route. Of all the passengers it was Dorothy who suffered the most from seasickness. But she suffered in other ways, too.

"Poor Mrs. Carey," Thomas wrote back to England. "She has had many fears and troubles, so that she was like Lot's wife, until we passed the Cape; but ever since, it seems too far to look back to Piddington that she turns her hopes and wishes to our safe arrival in Bengal."

Five months aboard ship with an infant and three boys aged four to eight would pose a challenge for any mother, but it was especially trying to Dorothy. Carey called his sons "complete sailors," but since he spent a good deal of time studying Bengali with Thomas, he may have had a tendency to overlook their behavior problems.

Dorothy must have sensed that she would probably never see England and loved ones again. She no doubt realized that people didn't last too long in India. Not sharing her husband's missionary commitment, she felt as if she were sailing toward a slow death.

The first year that the Careys spent in India did nothing to alleviate such fears. For both William and Dorothy it was a nightmare that they would never want to relive. If Dorothy had felt insecure due to William's frequent starts and stops around Piddington, think of how she must have felt around Calcutta.

First stop, Calcutta, November 1793: Upon arrival the Careys moved into the large home occupied by the Thomases. The expenses of the large home didn't seem to faze Thomas, but worried Carey, who wrote, they "filled my mind with anxiety and wretchedness." The life style of the European community in which they found themselves was fast-paced and hedonistic. The Careys felt out of place.

Second stop, Bandel, December 1793: Both the Careys and the Thomases moved to a smaller village, thirty miles north of Calcutta; financial problems continued to plague them. Creditors from Calcutta hounded Thomas, and Carey, now thoroughly disillusioned with his companion, wrote, "He is a very good man, but only fit to live at sea." Carey was hoping that both families could be self-sufficient by farming, but with debts piling up, he wasn't so sure. Thomas decided to move back to Calcutta and resume his medical practice; when Carey heard of a position available at Calcutta's Botanical Garden, he decided to move back there too.

Third stop, back in Calcutta, January 1794: The job at the Botanical Garden had been filled by the time Carey arrived. Unable to afford anything better, the Careys were forced to live in a marshy malarial area, where gangs of robbers roamed. They were now eating curry and rice, day in and day out—a far cry from what those in the European quarter were enjoying, and probably a far cry from what the Thomases themselves were eating. Carey scribbled in his diary: "My wife and sister too who do not see the importance of the mission as I do, are continuing exclaiming against me, and as for Mr. T., they think it very hard indeed that he should live in a city, in an affluent manner, and they be forced to go into a wilderness and live without many of what they call the necessaries of life, bread in particular." The haranguing of both Kitty and Dorothy seemed to be getting him down.

Soon Dorothy and the two oldest boys had dysentery; William, deeply concerned for his family's health but also frustrated by his inability to do any meaningful missionary work, was depressed. How could he learn Bengali when there were so many problems plaguing him? "If my family were but hearty in the work," he wrote, "I should find a great burden removed, but the carnal discourse of the passage and the pomp and grandeur of the Europeans here have intoxicated their minds, so as to make them unhappy in one of the finest countries in the world and lonely in the midst of a hundred thousand people."

Well, India is certainly a fine country, but the Careys were living in a malarial swamp. And while there may have been hundreds of thousands of people in Calcutta, they all spoke Bengali, a language that Dorothy would never be able to master.

Stop four, Debhatta, forty miles east of Calcutta, February 1794: William was offered some land rent-free, if he would clear it and build a house on it. All he needed were a few tools, some money to pay for transportation, and some seeds for a garden. Carey went to Thomas. Surely there must be some mission money remaining. There was none, and, of course, Thomas had plenty of financial troubles of his own. Seldom did Carey get discouraged, but this was an exception. "I am in a strange land," he wrote, "alone, no Christian friend, a large family and nothing to supply their needs."

William's discouragement did nothing to buoy Dorothy's spirits. Her depression deepened into neurosis. Carey wrote that she had "relapsed into her affliction and is much worse than she was before," indicating that it was not the first time for Dorothy to have such a relapse. Her sister naturally blamed William for everything. And William didn't know whom to blame. Sometimes he blamed Thomas. At other times he blamed himself. "I blame Thomas," he wrote, "for leading me into such expense at first, and I blame myself for being led."

He felt Job-like: "My temporal troubles remain just as they were. I have a place, but cannot remove my family to it, for want of money. Now all my friends are but One. I rejoice, however, that He is all-sufficient, and can supply all my wants spiritual and temporal. But why is my soul disquieted within me? Everything is known to God."

At times he wrote like David in the Psalms. He lamented that he didn't feel as close to God as he should. He described himself as "spiritually barren," "full of perplexity," and "at an awful distance from God." "Oh, what a shame," he wrote, "that I am not always satisfied with Him."

Finally, Carey received the money he needed, not from Dr. Thomas but from an Indian moneylender who charged him an exorbitant interest rate. Carey wasted no time getting his family on a boat upriver to Debhatta. For three days they traveled through an area teeming "with tigers, leopards, rhinoceros, deer, buffalo. No one dares to go on shore." Neither Dorothy nor Kitty had any confidence that Debhatta would be an improvement over Calcutta.

But near their destination, they found a hospitable Englishman—an answer to prayer—and while Carey cleared the land and started to build a house for his family, Dorothy, Kitty, and the children stayed with the Englishman. Actually, Kitty stayed there longer; she fell in love with her host and remained in Debhatta, thus reducing the Carey household by one. But in Carey's words, Dorothy was still "so ill."

Stop five, Malda, 250 miles north, March 1794: Carey hadn't made much progress in building his family a house in Debhatta when he got word from Thomas that in Malda, an indigo factory needed a manager for three months a year. The job paid well and the rest of the year would be his own for missionary activity. It sounded like another answer to prayer, or as Carey put it, "a remarkable opening in divine providence for our comfortable support."

Dorothy would have preferred staying in Debhatta near Kitty. It must have been an emotional farewell when the two sisters parted. This time the Carey family spent three weeks on the water as they plied their way up the river. It was the hottest time of the year, with mosquitoes everywhere, and Dorothy was in "a very weak state." Carey navigated the boat himself, which probably accounts for the three weeks it took to travel 250 miles. "Travelling," wrote Carey, "I have always found unfriendly to the progress of the divine life in my soul, but travelling with a family more particularly so."

Sixth stop, Dinadjpur, July 1794: The stop at Malda was brief. In Malda he learned a little about the indigo business; his salary would be about twenty-five pounds a month, and he and his family would have a large two-story house in which to live. Thomas would be managing a factory not far from Malda; the Careys would be located thirty-two miles north in the Dinadjpur district.

The Careys had made six moves in their first nine months on the mission field.

At last, Carey could devote a large part of his time to spreading the gospel.

But not quite yet.

In September he was stricken with malaria while Dorothy and their oldest son, Felix, were still suffering from dysentery. Then Peter, their five-year-old, also came down with dysentery. Within a few days he died.

William and Dorothy tried to find someone to dig Peter's grave, but the Hindus of the area refused. Finally, they contacted four Moslems who agreed to dig the grave but were unwilling to carry the body to it. Although they were too weak to do much, William and Dorothy were ready to do it themselves, when finally two servants consented to assist with the burial.

Peter was the third child that the Careys had

lost. But Dorothy thought she had lost everything. Kitty was left behind; Dorothy would never see her again. Once again Dorothy slipped into a depressed state. From this time on, William seldom referred to her in his writings. He spoke rather of his "domestic affliction."

Eight months later Carey wrote in his diary, "I have had very sore trials in my own family, from a quarter which I forebear to mention. Have greater need for faith and patience than ever I had."

No doubt he was referring to the fact that Dorothy had just written a secret letter to Dr. Thomas, telling him how William had been abusing her. Knowing Dorothy's mental state, Dr. Thomas didn't believe a word of it. Instead he replied to William, "You must endeavor to consider it a disease. . . . Were I in your case, I should be violent, but blessed be God, who suits our burdens to our backs. Think of Job; think of Jesus."

There were occasional glimmers of light for Dorothy. Baby Jonathan was born in 1796, when Dorothy was forty. It was their fifth son, along with two daughters, both of whom had died in infancy.

After the birth of Jonathan, William reported back to England, "We are well in health, except that my poor wife is in a very distressing state of mind; not maniacal, it is true, but afflicted . . . with 'ideal insanity.'" Probably Dorothy was retreating from her neurotic depression into flights of fantasy. Her heart was still in Piddington; probably her mind had a tendency to return there as well.

Later that year Carey wrote home regarding qualifications for future missionaries. One thing was that "it is absolutely necessary for the wives of missionaries to be as hearty in the work as their husbands." Previously, it hadn't dawned on William that this was so important. After all, merchants would go to the Orient with their wives, and no one asked how dedicated the wife might be to the rubber, cocoa, or tea business. But Carey was learning that it was different for missionaries.

As Dorothy became more and more isolated from society because of her mental illness, Carey grew in social grace and acceptance. In England he had been a cobbler and a village preacher. In India he was hobnobbing with the ruling and the merchant classes. At the same time, his missionary work was expanding; though not a single Indian had as yet accepted Jesus Christ as Savior and Lord, Carey had made some European converts.

A new day dawned for the missionary venture in 1799 when a fresh batch of eight missionaries arrived in Serampore, fourteen miles north of Calcutta. They wanted to join Carey but were refused permission. So Carey, now thirty-eight, and Dorothy, forty-four, joined them. It meant leaving the indigo business which had treated Carey well, but William knew of the advantages of a team of missionaries working together. Since one of the new missionaries was a printer and another a schoolteacher, it sounded like a good combination. It would also be helpful in dealing with the children and the problems of Dorothy.

When the Careys arrived at the new mission headquarters at Serampore, "Dorothy was so deranged that she was quite incapable of sharing in any of the domestic responsibilities." Hannah Marshman, one of the new workers, took the Carey boys under her wing, and not a year too soon. Dorothy had been unable to handle them, and William, even in his schoolteaching days, was not known as a disciplinarian. Mrs. Marshman wrote home to England about the situation: "Owing to Brother Carey's domestic affliction [meaning Dorothy], his perpetual avocations [probably gardening, or perhaps referring to Bible translation work] or perhaps an easiness of the temperament not wholly free from blame, his two oldest sons were left in great measure without control; hence obstinacy and self-will took a very deep root in their minds." Felix was fifteen; his brother, William, twelve.

Felix was the biggest problem, and Carey couldn't handle his own son. "The good man saw and lamented the evil but was too mild to apply an effectual remedy," wrote Mrs. Marshman candidly. "I could not see this without trembling for the consequences. . . . I thought that to refrain longer would be criminal." And Hannah Marshman waded in.

Hannah Marshman gets credit for providing the discipline, but the new missionary printer William Ward provided a combination big brother and surrogate father for Felix. At thirty, Ward was a little closer to Felix in age than was Felix's own father.

The transformation in the oldest Carey boy was amazing: "From being a tiger, he was transformed into a lamb." Within a year, young Felix was preaching his first sermon. Soon he became a valued member of the missionary team. In time, three of the four Carey boys became missionaries. The fourth, Jonathan, became an attorney of the Calcutta Supreme Court, serving also as treasurer of the Serampore mission. Apparently Mrs. Marshman and Mr. Ward arrived on the scene at exactly the right time.

It was partly through the witnessing of young Felix Carey that the first Indian was converted after William had been preaching and teaching for seven years. Carey was ecstatic: "Yesterday I had the happiness to desecrate the Ganges by baptizing the first Hindu and my son Felix."

Meanwhile, Dorothy grew worse. In 1801 Carey wrote: "Mrs. Carey is obliged to be constantly confined. She had long gotten worse and worse. But both fear of my own life and hers and the desire of the police of the place, obliged me to agree to her confinement." Because she was sometimes violent, she had to be confined to her room.

In 1804 Carey wrote home to England: "Poor Mrs. C. is rather worse than better. A very distressing object indeed. This affliction is heavy. Oh, may I bear it like a Christian, and may it be of benefit to me." Later, Carey wrote of her condition as being "maniacal."

Despite Carey's domestic distress, those early years in Serampore brought a string of successes. The New Testament was translated into Bengali, a church was formed, and Carey was appointed teacher and later professor of Oriental languages at the newly founded Fort William College in Calcutta. Carey could hardly believe it. Since he had only a sixth-grade education, he had to write back to England to find out how a college class should be conducted. But he was also amazed that he, a Dissenter, should be officially appointed by the governor-general. Carey's specialties in Oriental language were Sanskrit and Marathi, besides Bengali. Within ten years of his arrival in India, he had mastered all of them.

Then, late in 1807, at the age of fifty-one, Dorothy Carey passed away. She had been in India for fourteen years and had been somewhat deranged for nearly twelve of them. John Marshman wrote that he was amazed that William Carey could have accomplished so much in his "arduous biblical and literary labors . . . while an insane wife, frequently wrought up to a state of most distressing excitement, was in the next room, but one, to his study."

What caused Dorothy's mental illness? It may have been a hereditary weakness or problems caused by her early upbringing in the home of her parents in Piddington. Yet, undoubtedly the insecurity of living conditions both in England and in India accelerated Dorothy's decline. Perhaps even poor nutrition played a part. Though he disciplined himself like a hard taskmaster, William seems to have been easy-going and indecisive in his dealings with his family. He didn't provide the security and stability that Dorothy needed, so she lost confidence in him and her psychological fears were intensified. She needed a security which William couldn't provide physically and wouldn't provide emotionally.

Yet despite these apparent weaknesses as a husband, William Carey saw his sons grow up— though undisciplined at first—to love him and follow in his footsteps.

Six months after Dorothy died, William remarried. His bride was a Danish countess, Charlotte Rumohr. She was somewhat crippled and had come to Calcutta, of all places, for her health. Emotionally, culturally, and intellectually, she was the exact opposite of Dorothy. She had been introduced to Jesus Christ by Carey. The governor-general described the marriage as that of a learned and pious man and a Danish countess "whom he had converted from a Christian to a Baptist by very near drowning her in the ceremony of baptism."

It is difficult to know whether there had ever been any tenderness of emotion between Dorothy and William in the early years of their marriage. But there is no question about Charlotte's emotion toward William. "My dearest love," Charlotte wrote him, "I feel very much in parting with thee and feel very much in being so far from thee. . . . I cannot help longing for thee."

To Carey, Charlotte was everything a missionary's wife should be. After she died in 1821, Carey wrote a friend: "We had been married thirteen years and three weeks, during all which season, I believe, we had as great a share of conjugal happiness as ever was enjoyed by mortals. . . . My loss is irreparable."

Whatever else their marriage showed, it demonstrated that Carey could enjoy a successful marital relationship. In fact, Carey was so elated with the joys of his second marriage that he married a third time. Once again it was a happy marriage, ending with his own death eleven years later, in 1834.

By the time of his death he had translated the Bible into forty-four languages and dialects, had opened mission stations in India, Burma, and Bhutan, had established several schools, and had become an authority on horticulture and agriculture in India. Not bad for a plodder.

Yes, a plodder. Toward the end of his life, he said that if anyone should ever write his life story, he should "give me credit for being a plodder" and that "will describe me justly. I can plod. . . . To this I owe everything."

He would probably evaluate himself as a failure in business, in teaching, in the ministry, as a parent, and as a husband. But he succeeded because he continued plodding . . . and perhaps also because of his motto: "Expect great things from God; attempt great things for God."

It's very hard to evaluate Dorothy. In fact, no one really knows what went on inside her head during those twenty-six difficult years of marriage to William Carey. She probably had no estimation of his greatness nor his genius. Probably she was more concerned about the frequent moves—at least four in their thirteen years in England and seven in their thirteen years in India, not counting the boats and ships of various kinds on which they spent half a year. No doubt she would have been much happier at Piddington, where she had been born and reared by protective parents. Her health and her children's health were perpetual concerns; so was the scarcity of food. She didn't like the vegetable diet on which their poverty forced her to live in England, and she didn't appreciate the curry and rice diet in India.

Perhaps one of the rare clues to Dorothy's thinking comes in the names of two of her children. Most of their seven offspring were named after William's relatives. Two children, however, had unusual biblical names. One of these was certainly bestowed by Dorothy; probably the other one was also.

Felix had been born in 1785. *Felix* means "happy," and despite other uncertainties in her life, Dorothy was certainly glad to have had a son born to her. Ann, her first child, had died two years before, so the birth of Felix brought happiness.

The biblical Felix (Acts 26) was an indecisive man; Paul the missionary was trying to convince him of the Christian message, but Felix's unwillingness to antagonize the Jews delayed his response for two years. Dorothy, too, had a problem in making up her mind when Felix was born. Should she follow her husband and become a Baptist and break with her parents? She waited two years before allowing her husband to baptize her.

The next son that Dorothy probably named was Jabez. Jabez was born while William and Dr. Thomas were on a boat heading for India. Pressure was being placed on Dorothy to join her husband and do what a dutiful wife should do. But she couldn't do it. According to 1 Chronicles 4:9, Jabez's mother gave him that name, "because I bare him with sorrow." Dorothy's heart was also heavy.

In the next verse Jabez as an adult prayed to God to "enlarge my coast, and that thine hand might be with me, and that thou wouldest keep me from evil." For Dorothy to pray the prayer of Jabez meant that she, too, may have wanted God to "enlarge her coast." But she had inner struggles that were bigger than she could handle.

CHAPTER
THREE

Meet
Adoniram
and
Ann
Judson

The foreign missionary movement in America stems from the day that Adoniram and Ann Hasseltine Judson set sail for the land of Burma in 1812.

It was their honeymoon. They had been married one week earlier. The ship was strewn with chickens, pigs, chicken coops, and pigsties, and Adoniram was fastidious to a fault. Hardly the way to spend a honeymoon.

Besides that, they were both strong-minded and independent; so their marriage seemed to have two strikes against it before it got started.

But instead of striking out, their marriage made a big hit. And you have to ask the question, "Why?"

Why did this marriage succeed and the marriage of the Careys fail?

Certainly Adoniram was not an ideal husband, and as for Ann, she would have driven another man to distraction.

What, then, made this marriage work?

As a teenager, Nancy had a penchant for getting into trouble and then charming her way out of it. The townspeople thought that her liberal-minded father had spoiled her. After all, he had converted a large second-floor room into a dance hall. The Hasseltine ballroom soon became the social center for the town's young people, and you could be sure to find fun-loving Nancy at the center of things. Friends said that where she was, "no one can be gloomy or unhappy."

Most girls at the beginning of the nineteenth century received a very limited education, but Nancy's parents were determined that she should go further. Nancy, though undoubtedly quick-witted, was not a natural student; her social interests always seemed to get in the way.

Since Nancy was the youngest of four daughters, maybe it was to be expected that she should be pampered a bit, and especially after an older brother had been lost at sea. One biographer candidly says, "She certainly had a determination to get her own way. . . . Punishments and restraints brought no reform, nothing but resentful grief."

Sometimes she would leave the house and be gone for hours. Her mother was once heard to remark, "I hope one day you will be satisfied with rambling."

That was Nancy the rambler, charming but spoiled.

Then there was Don. Don was impetuous, brilliant, sometimes moody, and a bit eccentric. He had phobias against getting dirty and against saying good-bye. The son of a New England minister, he had learned to read when he was three years old. Although he was a bundle of wound-up energy, he always preferred books to play.

In a way, he admired his father, yet he was always rebelling against him. It was almost as if he were competing with him. Cocky, independent, and stubborn—determination was a family trait, just as evident in the father as in the son—he finished at the top of his college class and headed to New York City to seek fame and fortune as an actor and/or writer. He had renounced his father's belief in a personal God; his education had taken him beyond such primitive notions. And prayer, of course, was meaningless.

About the same time that Don was saying he was too educated to believe in prayer to a personal God, Nancy was saying, "If I'm old enough to attend balls, I am surely too old to say prayers."

You wouldn't think that God could make anything out of either of them, much less make them a couple who worked together beautifully. But that's what happened.

You see, Don and Nancy were only their nicknames. More properly they were called Adoniram Judson and Ann Hasseltine Judson, intrepid American missionaries to the land of Burma. Unlike the Careys, Adoniram and Ann were truly a missionary team.

The marriage between fun-loving, spoiled Ann and impetuous, stubborn Adoniram was not unending bliss, but it was remarkably compatible. They were a working team more than they were lovers, but what an effective team they were! The first Christian material published in Burma was a tract by Adoniram called *The Way to Heaven*; the second was a doctrinal piece written by Ann called *Mrs. Judson's Catechism*.

Just as William Carey is known as the father of British foreign missions, so Adoniram and Ann became the pioneers of American foreign missions. Ann also became a role model for thousands of women missionaries, not a millstone dragged to the mission field unwillingly, nor a passive servant of a missionary husband, but a co-missionary, part of the missionary team.

In the year 1806, in suburban Boston, where both of them grew up, you would never have guessed that either of them would be role models for anything, and certainly not for anything Christian.

Then, while reading a book by British reformer Hannah More, Ann was struck by this sentence: "She that liveth in pleasure is dead while she liveth." Sixteen-year-old Ann didn't like to be scolded by anyone, so she threw the book down and picked up Bunyan's *Pilgrim's Progress*. Within a few months, Ann, in her own words, "had passed from death into life."

Adoniram's conversion was not quite so simple. It was two years later that he was seeking a theatrical career in New York City. He had joined a traveling dramatic troupe which led "a reckless, vagabond life, finding lodgings where we could and bilking the landlord where we found opportunity—in other words running up a score and then decamping without paying the reckoning."

But twenty-year-old Adoniram didn't feel right about it. That certainly wasn't the way he wanted to spend the rest of his life. Disillusioned, he headed back to his home in Plymouth, Massachusetts, stopping for a night at a wayside inn. Adoniram had trouble sleeping that night, because a man in the next room was critically ill and moaning and groaning in pain. Obviously, his neighbor in the next room was dying. In the darkness of his room, Adoniram thought about the possibility of his own death and whether he was prepared for it. At times during the long hours he thought about returning to the Christian beliefs of his father, but then he imagined what his college chum Jacob Eames would say about his father's doctrines. And he waited for morning to come so that the terrors of the night would be forgotten.

Early the next morning, Adoniram went to the innkeeper. "That poor old man in the next room. How is he?" he asked.

"He passed away early this morning," came the reply. "And he wasn't old at all. He was a young man, about your age."

For some reason, Adoniram asked, "What was his name?" It was a rather stupid question, because Adoniram certainly didn't know anyone in that section of the country.

The innkeeper replied, "His name was Jacob Eames."

There was no mistaking the name or the identity. It was the young college friend whose religious skepticism had turned Adoniram against the religion of his father.

Dazed, he returned to Massachusetts and to his father. Echoing through his mind was the old word *Lost*. But it took three more months of intellectual struggle before he "made a solemn dedication of himself to God." It was December 2, 1808.

Remember that date, because that's when things started to happen in Adoniram's life. His father wanted him to enter the ministry and take a church in Massachusetts. Adoniram didn't want to. But the following fall he read a sermon about the need for missionaries in India and a book about the country of Burma. The idea captured his mind; in fact, he could think of little else. Neither ridicule nor common-sense reasoning could dampen his enthusiasm. He was stubbornly determined to be a missionary to either India or Burma, preferably the latter.

Of course, there were a few obstacles: No American mission boards existed and no American had ever gone out as a foreign missionary. The nearest mission board was in England, and the War of 1812 was looming. But what are a few minor obstacles to a dedicated and determined young man of twenty-two?

Undaunted, he found six other young men, and together they presented themselves to the New England Congregationalists for missionary service. And it was precisely on that day that he met Nancy (or Ann, whichever you prefer) Hasseltine over a deep-dish chicken pie and fell madly in love with her. He was never lukewarm about anything.

A month later he asked Nancy's father for her hand in marriage. Obviously, Adoniram was in a hurry. His letter to Mr. Hasseltine displays his spirit:

"I have now to ask whether you can consent to part with your daughter early next spring to see her no more in this world; whether you can consent to her departure and her subjection to the hardships and sufferings of a missionary life; whether you can consent to her exposure to the dangers of the ocean; to the fatal influence of the southern climate of India; to every kind of want and distress; to degradation, insult, persecution, and perhaps a violent death."

It was a nineteenth-century version of "telling it like it is."

Surprisingly, Hasseltine didn't say no to Adoniram. Instead he left the decision to Nancy. And not surprisingly, the girl who had lived for pleasure only a couple of years earlier didn't find it an easy decision to make. In her diary she asked herself whether she would be able to commit herself "entirely to God, to be disposed of, according to His pleasure."

Her sisters told her what they thought of Adoniram, and it wasn't all good. They acknowledged that he was single-minded and very religious, but he was also "by nature ardent, impetuous, and ambitious, with the most unshaken confidence in his own judgment, irrespective of the advice of his elders."

It was a package plan. She couldn't marry Adoniram without becoming a missionary to India, Burma, or some such place. So it was difficult to separate one decision from the other. But by October 1810 she succumbed to his wooing, if you can call it that. She wrote: "Jesus is faithful; His promises are precious. Were it not for these considerations, I should sink down in despair, especially as no female has, to my knowledge, ever left the shores of America to spend her life among the heathen."

Nancy the rambler accepted the challenge.

Adoniram, who had just turned twenty-two, was ecstatic about Nancy's acceptance of his proposal, but he was discouraged by the slow progress the New England Congregationalists were making toward raising financial support. So by year's end he was on a boat to London, hoping that he could convince the London Missionary Society to pitch in a few shillings toward their support. Perhaps he was thinking that he could shame the Americans into missionary support. Without a doubt, he was impetuous.

On his way he wrote Nancy: "With my whole heart I wish you, my love, a happy new year. . . . May every moment of the year bring you nearer to God and find you more prepared to hail the messenger of death as a deliverer and friend. . . . May this be the year in which you change your name, in which you take final leave of your relatives and native land; in which you will cross the wide ocean, and dwell on the other side of the world, among a heathen people." Hardly a typical love letter to one's fiancée.

1811 was a year when God taught Adoniram a lesson in patience, and that was not easy for him to learn. The British ship on which he was traveling to London was attacked by a French privateer, and the prospective missionary was taken prisoner to France. He knew Greek and Hebrew but not French, so he had difficulty convincing his captors that he was American, not British. Eventually he got to London where he found that the London Missionary Society would not consent to a joint venture with an American board. Perhaps if he and Nancy would become British missionaries instead of American missionaries, they could gain support in London.

Back in America that fall, Adoniram squabbled with his own board. "If you will not send me," he shouted at them, "I will become a British missionary." The ultimatum was not appreciated. But finally, one of the board members—there's alway a peacemaker in every crowd—said that young Adoniram had an excess of self-reliance that got him into trouble working as a team member, but it would stand him in good stead on the mission field. And with surprising speed, the necessary support was raised.

February 1812 was the big month. In fact, it's difficult to imagine how Adoniram and Nancy could pack so much into a few days.

Wednesday, February 5, Bradford, Massachusetts: Adoniram Judson, twenty-three, and Ann Hasseltine, twenty-two, were married in the west room of Deacon Hasseltine's house.

Thursday, February 6, Salem, Massachusetts: Adoniram, along with four other men, were "publicly set aside for the service of God in the

Gospel of His Son, among the Heathen." It was an emotional ordination service attended by nearly two thousand people. As the young men were being ordained, Nancy, wearing her new scoop bonnet, walked quietly down the aisle and knelt near her husband. She, too, was becoming a missionary.

Monday, February 10, Salem harbor: After a farewell service the previous night, Adoniram and Nancy boarded their ship for India. "It looks like Noah's ark," Ann said when she saw all the chicken coops and pig pens aboard. Due to weather delays it wasn't for another week, however, that the ship finally set sail. That week—their honeymoon—they spent waiting anxiously in the home of a friend in Salem.

During those few days in February, Nancy learned about some of her husband's idiosyncracies—such as his phobia against saying good-bye. On the morning after their marriage he got her to leave her home in Bradford before dawn, so he wouldn't have to say good-bye to her family. On the night of the huge ordination service, he again tried to get away quickly; this time they were thwarted in their escape attempt and were brought back to shake hands with the crowd.

In Salem when they were finally informed that their ship was ready to embark, they were staying in a home filled with friends. "Without a word to anyone, he slipped quietly out of the house, walked alone down the snowy street to the wharf, found a boat and went on board the *Caravan*. Here he waited for Nancy," according to biographer Courtney Anderson, who also records, "Nancy was distressed. . . ."

You can imagine the emotions going through Nancy's mind as the ship left port. After two weeks of incredible excitement, it was an emotional letdown. On board ship she confessed that she "had many distressing apprehensions of death" and "felt unwilling to die on the sea, not so much on account of my state after death, as the dreadfulness of perishing amid the waves."

But then she began to enjoy the voyage. To get exercise, Adoniram and Nancy skipped rope and danced. Because of the crowded decks, they couldn't do much walking or running.

And she got better acquainted with the strange, impetuous, brilliant young man she had married. In her journal, she wrote that she had found Adoniram to be "one of the kindest, most faithful and affectionate of husbands."

But before long some problems developed.

It all started when Adoniram began studying his Greek New Testament and analyzed the Greek word for "baptism." As a Congregationalist he had in infancy been sprinkled with a few drops of water on his head. Now his study of the Greek language and his consideration of biblical practice increasingly convinced him that baptism should be by immersion.

When he shared his thoughts with Nancy, she

was alarmed—and for good reason. They were Congregational missionaries sent out by the Congregational board. Church leaders had worked long and hard to raise enough money to support the Judsons. It would be thoughtless and downright impractical to change beliefs now. They would be left without a mission board. You don't change horses in the middle of the stream, and you don't change mission boards in the middle of the ocean.

"I tried to have him give it up," Nancy wrote later, "and rest satisfied in his old sentiments, and frequently told him if he became a Baptist, I would not." That shows that Nancy had a mind of her own.

"He, however, said he felt it his duty to examine closely a subject on which he felt so many doubts" and "was determined to read candidly and prayerfully, and to hold fast or embrace the truth, however mortifying, however great the sacrifice."

Even after their ship had landed in Calcutta, the discussion on baptism continued, and it didn't help Nancy's Congregational position to be living among British Baptists and to be hobnobbing with William Carey, the pioneer Baptist missionary.

But Nancy wouldn't go down without a struggle. To defend her own position, she spent two or three days comparing the Old and New Testaments on the subject. "I intend to persevere in examining the subject, and hope that I shall be disposed to embrace the truth, whatever it may be. It is painfully mortifying to my natural feelings to think seriously of renouncing a system which I have been taught from infancy, and respect and embrace one which I have been taught to despise."

Such psychological factors did not faze Adoniram, who cherished his independence, but gregarious Nancy was bothered about being isolated from relatives and friends, and especially from the missionary colleagues who had accompanied them to India. "If he should renounce his former sentiments," she wrote, "he must offend his friends at home, hazard his reputation, and, what is still more trying, be separated from his missionary associates." Nancy dreaded the implications.

It was early in August that Adoniram reached his decision to become a Baptist. Nancy struggled with the issue longer, but by the end of the month she, too, felt that the weight of the scriptural arguments were on the side of the Baptists. The next month Adoniram and Nancy were baptized by immersion by one of William Carey's associates. In her journal Nancy wrote what the decision meant emotionally: "We feel that we are alone in the world, with no real friend but each other, no one on whom we can depend but God."

The Judsons had other problems, too, the biggest of which was how to get to Burma from

India. Their idealistic notions of Burma were dashed; the source book on Burma was found to be totally unreliable. The British missionaries in India told them bluntly that Burma would be both impossible to enter and impossible to live in.

To complicate the situation, the British authorities in India didn't like missionaries, especially American ones. The Judsons were ordered to be deported to England. Feeling they had a higher calling, the Judsons jumped ship and hitchhiked aboard another vessel to the island of Mauritius, a little French island about twenty-five miles square and 3500 miles southwest in the middle of the Indian Ocean.

The longer they were on Mauritius, the more they realized that being there wasn't their calling either. To add to their complications Nancy was pregnant.

Adoniram, whose moods sometimes got the better of him, was getting discouraged. They had left New England in February 1812; now it was June 1813, and they were still 4000 miles from Burma. Mauritius was not exactly Grand Central Station; boats going anywhere, much less to Burma, were a rarity. And, of course, with all they had heard about Burma, it must have crossed their minds that maybe the whole thing was an impetuous mistake. After all, Adoniram had made impetuous mistakes before.

And then a ship pulled into the harbor bound for—of all places—Rangoon, Burma. Now the complication was that Nancy was eight months pregnant. Should they pass up the opportunity and return to England as the British authorities had ordered? Some advised them to postpone their missionary debut for a few years: "A few years lost are better than losing all to no purpose in the living hell of Burma."

As always, Nancy and Adoniram talked it over. The old idealism of their youth had now evaporated; this was serious business. But she and Adoniram were still determined to go to Burma, come what may.

At this point Nancy was not expecting great results: "We cannot expect to do much, in such a rough uncultivated field; yet, if we may be instrumental in removing some of the rubbish, and preparing the way for others, it will be a sufficient reward. I have been accustomed to view this field of labor, with dread and terror; but I now feel perfectly willing to make it my home the rest of my life."

Adoniram was concerned about Nancy's physical condition, so he hired a European woman to serve as a nurse for her on the voyage to Rangoon. But as the nurse stepped aboard the ship, she slipped and fell to the deck and died.

After struggling unsuccessfully to save the woman's life, Nancy went into a state of shock herself. A few days out to sea, Nancy gave birth to her first child; it was stillborn. No physician or nurse was aboard; only Adoniram was available to attend his wife. Later, Nancy said that she owed her life to her husband.

When they arrived in Rangoon, Nancy was hardly in the frame of mind and certainly not in physical health to begin her missionary service. Their first impression of Burma, which they had dreamed about for so long, was that it was "dark, cheerless and unpromising."

Despite the circumstances, the Judsons began immediately to learn the language. At first the Hindu scholar who agreed to teach Adoniram refused to instruct Nancy because, as she put it, "it was rather beneath him to instruct a female. . . . But when he saw I was determined to persevere, and that Mr. Judson was as desirous that he should instruct me as himself, he was more attentive." Once that hurdle was over, they spent twelve hours a day in language study.

A year later she described her daily schedule this way: "My mornings are busily employed in giving directions to the servants, providing food for the family, etc. I have many more interruptions than Mr. Judson, as I have the entire management of the family. This I took on myself for the sake of Mr. Judson's attending more closely to the study of the language, yet I have found that it is the most direct way I could have taken to acquire the language; as I am frequently obliged to speak Burmese all day. I can talk and understand others better than Mr. Judson, though he knows more about the nature and construction of the language."

Besides the language, Nancy also picked up the local customs, even adopting the dress style of the local women. The one custom she never followed was wearing Burmese sandals.

The work was slow, hard, and lonely. There were no European or American women to be Nancy's friends, and it took three years for the first packet of letters from America to arrive. Adoniram had a very satisfying conversation with his Burmese teacher about Christianity, but there were still no converts. A child born in 1815 (named Roger Williams Judson) was a joy to Nancy and Adoniram. Then, suffering from a cough and fever, he suddenly died at eight months. The funeral had to be held within hours, and the small body was buried among the mango trees in the garden of the mission house.

In her sorrow, Nancy launched a school for Burmese girls, wrote a simple catechism in Burmese, and began translating the Book of Jonah because she thought it would be easy to translate.

Five years went by with still no converts. Plenty of tracts, catechisms, and portions of Scripture. Weekly classes and counseling sessions. But no converts.

If one Hindu would step over the line, Adoniram was sure that others would follow. But how to get that first one—that was the question.

Perhaps if he could import a few Indian Christians who lived on the Burmese border, their example would provide the needed nudge. It would take only a few weeks of travel for Adoniram, a few weeks away from Nancy, to talk the Indian Christians into visiting Burma with him. At least, that's what he thought.

Not long after Adoniram left, Nancy was engulfed in trouble. First came word from the Burmese viceroy that all foreign teachers were to be banished; then came a cholera epidemic followed by the rumor that the British would soon invade Burma, a rumor that didn't endear missionaries to the Burmese officials.

A missionary printer and his wife had joined the Judsons by this time, but the printer now decided that he could do his printing more effectively in India. After Adoniram's absence had stretched to seven months, Nancy got word that his ship was missing at sea.

Should she join the missionary printer and his wife? What future was there for her in Burma?

She decided to board the next vessel for India. Then she changed her mind. If Adoniram should return and find her missing, what would he do? No matter what the printer did, Nancy intended to stay in Burma, keep on with her studies, and "leave the event to God."

It was a wise decision.

Not long afterward, Adoniram came home. The joy of his return, Nancy wrote, "more than compensates for the months of dejection and distress which his long absence has occasioned. Now I feel ashamed of my repinings, my want of confidence in God and resignation to His will. I have foolishly thought, because my trials were protracted, they would never end, or rather that they would terminate in some dreadful event."

Yes, Nancy was human.

In 1818 two new missionary couples arrived in Burma; one of the wives found the living conditions unbearable. What she meant was that she had a hard time living with Nancy. "It could well have been true," says one biographer, "that Adoniram and Nancy ran things with a high hand." The Judsons had survived in Burma for five years and had a few ideas on how a mission should operate. The idealistic neophyte missionaries would have to adjust.

Perhaps Adoniram was impatient or perhaps he was prodded by the presence of the younger exuberant missionaries, but when a new emperor took the Burmese throne in the legendary capital city of Ava, it was agreed that the time had come to ask for royal permission to teach Christianity to the king's subjects. If he said yes, the door would be wide open for the Judsons and others; if he said no, at least they could leave their writings behind as they sailed away.

But there was a disagreement in the Judson home. Adoniram thought he should be accompanied on the historic visit to the king by one of the male missionaries who had just joined them. Nancy disagreed. She felt she not only could speak the Burmese language fluently but could also use her demonstrated ability to twist potentates around her fingers. Maybe Nancy also remembered the last time her husband had left her on a trip that was supposed to have taken only a few weeks.

But Adoniram said no, and one day before Nancy's thirtieth birthday, her husband and his fellow missionary Colman began their trek to visit the emperor at Ava, the seat of the "Golden Presence," as it was called.

Maybe Nancy was right after all. Six weeks later Adoniram and Colman returned with their heads hanging low. They had failed to get the emperor's OK. Adoniram was glum: "I could moralize half an hour on the apt resemblance, the beautiful congruity, between the desolate state of our feelings and the sandy barren surface of this miserable beach. But "tis idle all.' Let the beach and the sorrow go together. Something better will turn up tomorrow."

It did.

There were new converts now, and they were less discouraged about the news than Adoniram. He feared that they might fall away from the faith. Instead, their faith grew stronger and more new converts were added.

However, all was not so well with Nancy. A liver ailment grew progressively worse. The only place where she could receive adequate treatment was in America. So this time it was Nancy's turn to leave and Adoniram's turn to stay behind.

He was never good at saying good-bye. He tried to joke about it, but his true feeling for Nancy came through clearly: "It is said that man is prone to jest in the depths of misery; and the bon mots of the scaffold have been collected. . . . I feel as if I was on the scaffold and signing as it were my own death warrant. I have been occupied in making up my mind to have my right arm amputated and my right eye extracted . . . in order to prevent a decay and mortification of the whole body conjugal."

In her absence, he busied himself in translating the New Testament. When she returned twenty-eight months later, she was well again. In his words, she was "the Ann Hasseltine of other days." His happiness was "inexpressible."

They had a lot of news to share with each other. Nancy had spent time in London, Boston, Baltimore, Calcutta, and points in between; had finished a book manuscript, *An Account of the American Baptist Mission to the Burman Empire*; and had seen a myriad of old friends and relatives.

Adoniram's big news for Nancy was that he had visited the emperor in Ava once again and that the emperor had invited them to come and live in the capital city. Despite their attachment to Rangoon, the opportunity was too good to pass up. Two months later, they moved to a little three-room home in Ava. Though the house was built on stilts to allow air movement, the 108 degree (Fahrenheit) heat of the stifling summer was still unbearable.

But unbearable heat was the least of their problems. Just as they had completed their move, word came that the British army was preparing to invade Burma. This time it was no idle rumor. And the Burmese, most of whom had never seen a white man before, had trouble distinguishing between Americans and Englishmen.

Within six months of their move to Ava, Adoniram was hauled off to prison, where he was bound with three pairs of ankle fetters to a block of granite. In the windowless prison, he was overwhelmed with heat, and gagged on the indescribable stench. His clothing was shredded, his face was covered with mud, and for Adoniram, who treasured cleanliness next to godliness, it was traumatic.

Understandably, Adoniram was thrown into depression. Biographer Courtney Anderson tells what was going through his mind: "What had he brought to those who depended on him? Nothing but death. Death for his only son. Now death for himself, probably death for Nancy. And what was there to show for it? Eighteen converts in the twelve years since he had left Salem. Of those, probably only a few would remain faithful—if they survived. Eighteen souls for all those years and lives. And the Burmese New Testament. But most of that was in manuscript, in the little wooden house by the river. Almost certainly it would be destroyed or lost."

Enterprising Nancy was doing everything she could. First, she had been summoned before the magistrate and interrogated. He got nowhere with her. The next day Nancy was able to smuggle food into the prison and began a letter-writing campaign to the emperor's sister (Nancy had an "in" with her). She wrote a petition to the empress and then tried to get permission to visit her husband.

She finally accomplished the latter by bribing a prison official. She almost wished she hadn't been successful. A British prisoner who was in the same jail described the reunion: "Two days in prison had turned the most fastidious man she knew into a haggard, unshaven scarecrow, his usually spotless white starched neckcloth a filthy rag, his neat black broadcloth suit dissheveled, torn and smeared with fragments of rotting plantain leaves. She could scarcely recognize him. She gave him one long horrified incredulous look and hid her face in her hands."

Nancy couldn't succumb to weakness now. She would need divine strength and wisdom to cope, for she couldn't let Adoniram down. She knew that soldiers would soon be at her house confiscating everything of value, including Adoniram's translation of the Bible into Burmese. He had spent years in preparing it; she couldn't allow it to be destroyed.

She went into her small backyard, dug two holes, and buried the family silver in one and the Burmese Bible in the other. A few hours later, the soldiers came and went away empty-handed.

Nancy's next priority was to rouse her husband out of his depression. He needed encouragement and something to occupy his mind. The way to provide both was to try to devise ways of communicating to each other without the prison guards knowing it. Sometimes Nancy wrote notes on little cakes that she buried in bowls of rice; at other times she put notes in the long nose of a teapot which she brought to the prisoners. Adoniram could never be sure when or how the next note from his wife might appear. In response, he devised a system of writing on tile which was invisible when the tile was wet, but was legible to Nancy when it dried off.

Of course, all of Nancy's hectic efforts were looked upon with extreme suspicion by the authorities. Frequently she was summoned to court. Such occasions became a challenge for her, and God supplemented her natural gift of being able to think on her feet with wisdom of the Spirit.

She knew that Adoniram's Bible translation couldn't stay buried in her backyard for long. For one thing, her husband was worrying about it too much; for another, the dampness of the soil would soon start to affect it and it would soon rot. So, in a rather daring operation, she smuggled the hefty manuscript to Adoniram in prison. He had asked the guards for a pillow, and the next day Nancy came to the prison with his request. The pillow was a bit heavy, rather bulky, and too hard for the normal comfort of most people, but Adoniram rested easy upon it, knowing that it contained his Burmese manuscript.

About this time, Nancy, now thirty-four, discovered she was pregnant once again. Her frantic pace had to slow down, although not by much. And in January 1825, seven months after Adoniram's arrest, Maria Elizabeth Judson was born. Ten years before, she had given birth to Roger Williams Judson, who lived only eight months. The place and the time were less propitious than ever for a baby to be born.

Shortly after Maria Elizabeth was born, Nancy resumed both her daily walks to the prison (with her babe in arms) to smuggle messages to her husband and her regular visits to the governor's house to beg for her husband's release.

After eleven months in prison, Adoniram was moved. He thought he was going to be assassinated, but the move was to a new location about four miles away. Some of the prisoners, "skin-covered skeletons, clothed in rags," collapsed on their march. Adoniram survived, but on reaching the destination, he fell into an unconscious stupor. The first voice to rouse him the next day was Nancy's. She had discovered that the prisoners were being moved and so had come with little Maria as quickly as she could.

Barely conscious, Adoniram whispered, "Why have you come? I hoped you would not follow. You cannot live here."

But Nancy did. For months she and Maria lived in a little room nearby that also served as a grain bin.

When the British troops came and liberated them in November 1825, Adoniram was in better physical shape than Nancy. Smallpox and then cerebral spinal meningitis had taken their toll. Her hair had been shaved off; her head and feet were covered with blisters. The Burmese thought that she was dead, but she rallied.

The general of the liberating British army honored the Judsons with a ceremonial dinner, but shortly thereafter Nancy was stricken with another fever. This time she couldn't fight it. She died at the age of thirty-six.

Adoniram continued his work in Burma for twenty-four more years. His translation of the Bible was published, and sixty-three churches were established in his lifetime.

Eight years after Nancy's death, he married Sarah Boardman, the widow of another missionary. She was different from Nancy, "calmer, less dominant, with less fire, but perhaps more glow,"

but like Nancy she was intelligent and courageous. After eleven years of marriage and eight
children, she died.

Judson's third wife was also a remarkable
woman. Emily Chubbock, who wrote children's
books under the pen name of Fanny Forester,
was a high school teacher with wit, charm, and a
spirited personality. Adoniram was nearly sixty
when he met her, and she was not quite thirty. He
had no intention of marrying her. He had contacted her about the possibility of writing a
biography of his second wife, Sarah. He ended
up marrying her. A storm of criticism mounted:
why should a dedicated missionary marry a pro-
fessional woman who wrote stories for secular
magazines? But Judson seldom let criticism bother
him. Together Adoniram and Emily, alias Fanny
Forester, returned to Burma to serve as missionaries. Four years later, Adoniram completed his
pilgrimage and went to be with the Lord.

All three of Adoniram's wives were strong,
somewhat determined women, even as he was
independent. But Ann Hasseltine Judson is the
wife who set the pattern for future missionaries
and who provided Adoniram with a strong dedicated co-worker whom he could count on and
respect as an equal.

Maybe that was their secret. They respected
and honored each other, despite their idiosyncracies. Though they often worked as a team, each

gave the other space to develop independently. They had no better friends than each other.

Each possessed character traits that could have torn the marriage apart. Instead, they worked together to make it strong.

CHAPTER
FOUR

Meet
Calvin
and
harriet
Stowe

W ho's Calvin Stowe?" you ask. He's the husband of Harriet Beecher Stowe, the celebrated author of *Uncle Tom's Cabin*. She was descended from the famous Beecher family in New England. According to Abraham Lincoln, she started the Civil War. She lectured in England as well as in the United States, and wrote scores of magazine articles and many books.

But you're still asking, "Who's Calvin?"

Well, I'd like to introduce him to you.

It took something for a nineteenth-century man to be married to a famous career woman.

But what was that something?

What was the glue that kept these two people— who often criticized each other—from separating?

At first, you'll be impressed with Harriet. After all, she was a remarkable woman with a quick wit. But gradually, you'll come to enjoy Calvin, too.

"My dear husband, I have been thinking of all your trials, and I really pity you in having such a wife. I feel as if I had been only a hindrance to you instead of a help, and most earnestly and daily do I pray to God to restore my health that I may do something for you and my family. I think if I were only at home I could at least sweep and dust, and wash potatoes."

It is doubtful, however, whether Hattie Stowe would have done much sweeping and dusting even if she had been home.

In her later books, Harriet Beecher Stowe wrote of "ministering daily in holy works" and of redeeming "common toils from grossness and earthliness." But she wasn't always successful in taking her own advice.

Once when her husband was away, she wrote him, "I am already half sick with confinement to the house." And a year later when Calvin Stowe was at a ministers' convention, she told him, "I am sick of the smell of sour milk, and sour meat, and sour everything, and then the clothes *will* not dry, and no wet thing does, and everything smells mouldy; and altogether I feel as if I never wanted to eat again."

At times she sounds more like a frustrated Erma Bombeck than a woman who was supposed to be able to redeem "common toils from grossness and earthliness."

Calvin Stowe was not exactly Mr. Handyman-around-the-house either. Awkward and inept, he was often overcome by his moods. A hypochondriac who sometimes slid into depression and hopelessness, he was known to go to his room and sulk for hours.

Hattie's fame as America's great novelist of the nineteenth century overshadowed Calvin's role as a seminary professor. She was acclaimed by literary and political figures on both sides of the Atlantic from Dickens to Twain and from Queen Victoria to Lincoln. Lincoln suggested that she was the one who actually started the Civil War. And Calvin? At times you could find him tagging along behind her on lecture tours or on the banquet circuit.

In his own field he was an erudite scholar, and Hattie was proud of him, but most people didn't see him in that setting. To tell the truth, even many of Hattie's biographers saw him as "gluttonous, neurasthenic, timid and lazy, a scatter-brain in emergencies and quite devoid of that talent for getting things done."

Maybe so, but the Stowes had a surprisingly

strong marriage, glued together by love and two delightful senses of humor.

Hattie's *Uncle Tom's Cabin* became a runaway best-seller. More than 100,000 copies were sold in six months, and Hattie was catapulted overnight to the forefront of America's abolition movement. Basically, she was not a wild-eyed radical, but a mild-mannered moderate crusader, even as her minister father, Lyman, had been before her.

Lyman Beecher, a Congregational minister in Litchfield, Connecticut, had intoned against dueling, drinking, and Unitarianism, and thought that the slavery issue would best be solved by regeneration instead of by abolition. He had views on almost everything, including the birth of his sixth child in 1811. He told everyone that he wished it had been a boy. It turned out to be Harriet.

Her redeeming quality was that she was brilliant—he called her a genius when she was six— and her mind was honed by the subjects that were table conversation in the Beecher household. Her father beamed when at age twelve she wrote an essay, "Can the Immortality of the Soul be Proved by the Light of Nature?"

Hattie was small and bookish. She loved the poetry of Lord Byron and idolized the poet, but that was about the naughtiest thing in her life. In personality she was puzzling: sometimes moody and withdrawn, often witty and carefree, and introspective to an extreme. Yet she was a good listener, able to empathize deeply with others.

The Beecher family was a close-knit group of individualists. Hattie's oldest sister, Catherine, had launched a girls' school in Hartford. At thirteen, Hattie attended Catherine's school for one year, then taught Latin to younger students the next.

And that turned out to be a big year in Hattie's life. For one thing, Lord Byron died. That crushed her. She was recovering from her sorrow when she returned home the following summer to sit under her father's preaching. Throughout New England Lyman Beecher was getting a reputation as a spellbinding preacher. Normally, Hattie wasn't impressed; nor was he. "The less I have to say," he admitted, "the more I holler."

And Hattie said, "Most of my father's sermons were as unintelligible to me as if he had spoken in Choctaw."

But one Sunday was different. Perhaps because he couldn't decipher the scribbled notes which he had crumpled and stuffed into his pockets, he spoke extemporaneously. His text was the words of Christ: "Behold, I call you no longer servants, but friends." Hattie was "drawn to listen by a certain pathetic earnestness in his voice."

Hattie responded. That afternoon, she fell down on her knees in her father's study and sobbed, "Father, I have given myself to Jesus and He has taken me."

Sister Catherine, who had struggled against God for months before yielding, was dubious of the ease at which Hattie had made her decision. She was amazed, she said, that "a lamb could so easily be brought into the fold without being chased all over the lot by the shepherd."

Hattie's struggles lay ahead of her. She felt she was good for nothing, a feeling that plagued her until she wrote *Uncle Tom's Cabin*. At age fifteen, she wrote Catherine, "I don't know as if I am fit for anything, and I have thought that I could wish to die young, and let the remembrance of me and my faults perish in the grave, rather than live, as I fear I do, a trouble to everyone. You don't know how perfectly wretched I often feel: so useless, so weak, so destitute of all energy. Mama often tells me that I am a strange, inconsistent being."

Strange and inconsistent she was. At twenty-one, though she was a "handsome young woman of medium height and a slender, graceful figure," she had no suitors. She spent too much time reading and studying and daydreaming; her family thought she spent too much time "owling about."

She, too, was concerned about her lack of friends. "Do you think," she asked an older brother, "that there is such a thing as so realizing the presence and character of God that He can supply the place of earthly friends?"

In her twenty-first year, she made a resolution to emerge from her shell. "Instead of shrinking into a corner, I am holding out my hand and forming acquaintances with all who will be acquainted with me."

It was a good year to make such a resolution, for that was the year that her father, Lyman Beecher, was invited to become president of Lane Theological Seminary in Cincinnati, Ohio. That fall the family went west, throwing gospel tracts out the window of the stage coach as they traveled.

Catherine was there too, and in a few months she had begun a new school for the young women of Cincinnati, called the Western Female Seminary. When Catherine saw there was a need for a geography book, she asked Hattie to write it. Within a few months, Hattie wrote her first book, but the intense pressure of meeting the deadline left her with morbid feelings again. "Thought, intense emotional thought, has been my disease. . . . My mind is exhausted and seeks to be sinking into deadness. . . . Thought is pain and emotion is pain."

Then some new friends came into her life. In August 1833, Calvin Stowe, newly appointed professor of biblical literature, came to Cincinnati with his bride, Eliza, who soon became Hattie's best friend. The three joined a literary group called the Semi-Colon Club; Hattie timidly submitted some of her stories to the Club and was thrilled with the encouragement she received.

A year later Eliza Stowe died in a cholera

epidemic. Hattie was heartbroken, almost as grief-stricken as the widower Calvin Stowe. They consoled each other in their sorrow.

Like Hattie, Calvin was a New Englander. His father had died when Calvin was only six, and he was raised by "an anxious, fretful mother and two strong-minded spinster aunts." Calvin bore the psychological marks for the rest of his life. Somehow he scraped together enough money to get to college. Four years later he graduated as valedictorian. His reputation as a Hebrew scholar grew rapidly, and while still in his late twenties, he was named to the faculty of Lyman Beecher's seminary in Cincinnati.

Prince Charming for Hattie would probably have been a cross between the dashing literary Lord Byron and her virtuous preacher-father. At first glance, Calvin Stowe bore no resemblance to either; yet, he had an interest in literature, and was a good preacher and an outstanding scholar. Most biographers, however, describe him as "round and rumpled, plump and balding, moon-faced and absent-minded, short and stocky, timid and lazy, and a scatterbrain in emergencies as well."

Years later Mark Twain's daughter, Susy Clemens, saw him and ran home to tell her father, "Santa Claus has got loose."

Even Hattie had to laugh at some of Calvin's idiosyncracies. She once wrote to a friend, tongue-in-cheek, that Calvin was "of Goblin origin decidedly, probably he preexisted in Germany, and certainly it was a great mistake that he was born in America."

Fortunately, Calvin had a sense of humor, too.

At first he was attracted to Hattie because she enjoyed talking to him about his departed wife. But he was also attracted to the Beecher home, which, while not elegant, was adorned with taste, witty and pious conversation, and familial love. He had never known a family like that before.

Hattie, of course, was flattered that a distinguished young professor, eight years her senior, should be interested in her. One incident seemed to weld their relationship. One day only a few months after Eliza's death, Lyman Beecher, Hattie, and Calvin Stowe attended a presbytery meeting at a minister's home overlooking the Ohio River, not far from Cincinnati. They noticed that the minister lit a lantern and hung it in his window at night. When they asked the reason, he explained that any slave living across the river in Kentucky would know by the lantern in the window that he could find food and clothing in this home if he dared to escape from his master. Then the minister told stories of slaves he had helped, including a young Negro mother who had attempted to cross the Ohio River as it was beginning to thaw. Her baby was bundled to her breast. A March thaw made the crossing perilous; cracks formed in the ice. A thin film of water covered the surface, and she didn't know if the ice would support her next step. She slipped and fell, then struggled up, only to slip and fall again. Finally she reached the Ohio shore, climbed the steep bluff to the minister's home, and found food and dry clothing inside.

It was a story that neither Hattie nor Calvin would ever forget.

What cemented the relationship between the two of them was a series of evening messages preached by Calvin. Hattie took the assignment of reporting on the sermons for the Cincinnati newspaper. To make sure she had all the points of the message stated accurately, she met with Calvin both before and after each message.

About a year after Eliza's death, Calvin proposed to Hattie. A few months later—in January 1836—they were married; she was twenty-four; he was thirty-two.

On her wedding day she wrote a friend in New England, "Well, about half an hour more and your old friend, companion, schoolmate, etc., will cease to be Hattie Beecher and change to nobody knows who. . . . I have been dreading and dreading the time and lying awake all last week wondering how I should live through this overwhelming crisis, and lo, it has come and I feel nothing at all."

Three weeks later, she continued her play-by-play account of her marriage: "My dear, it is a wonder to myself. I am tranquil, quiet and happy."

Of course, she had to get used to Calvin. Since

he was inept at hammering and sawing, she had to learn to do some things for herself. But his lack of physical dexterity didn't cause her to look down on him. It was obvious that she had married a brilliant man who was going places in the academic world.

Their wedding trip had been to a convention where he spoke on methods of Prussian education. Five months later he was off to Europe, thanks to a grant from the Ohio legislature (with the prodding of William Henry Harrison) to do research on education in Europe.

Before he returned, Hattie (who used her given name of Harriet more and more) bore twins named Eliza Tyler Stowe (after Calvin's first wife) and Harriet Beecher Stowe. A third child, Henry Ellis, was born a year later.

Thus, within two years of marriage, she had three children. She described her day: "Up I jump and up wakes baby. 'Now little boy, be good and let mother dress, because she is in a hurry.' I get my frock half on and baby by that time has kicked himself down off his pillow and is crying and fisting the bed clothes in great order. I stop with one sleeve off and one on to settle matters with him. Having planted him bolt upright and gone all up and down the chamber barefoot to get pillow and blankets to prop him up, I finish putting my frock on and hurry down to satisfy myself that breakfast is in progress. Then back I come into the nursery, where remembering that it is washing day and that there is a great deal of work to be done, I apply myself vigorously to sweeping, dusting and setting-to-rights so necessary where there are three little mischiefs always pulling down as fast as one can put up."

With three mischievous children and one absent-minded husband, Harriet had enough on her mind, but other problems were closing in. Economic problems were threatening the seminary, and the slavery question was embroiling the city of Cincinnati in civil unrest.

Calvin fretted. Harriet seemed almost oblivious to the outside problems: "I am but a mere drudge with few ideas beyond babies and housekeeping."

The longer they were married, the more they realized how different they were. Calvin put it this way: "I am naturally anxious, to the extent of needlessly taking much thought beforehand. You are hopeful to the extent of being heedless of the future, thinking only of the present." Calvin moped while Harriet hoped.

Calvin's mother came to help with the children, but she didn't help the marriage. She criticized Harriet for being extravagant with expenses and for wanting to be waited on. According to Harriet, her mother-in-law kept up "a perpetual state of complaint," until Calvin began to view his wife in "a wrong light."

As Calvin's salary checks became slimmer and slimmer, Harriet decided to write some magazine articles and submit them to Eastern publications. Her success was immediate. "I have realized enough by writing one way and another to enable me to add to my establishment a stout German girl who does my housework, leaving Anna full time to attend to the children, so I have about three hours per day in writing and if you see my name coming out everywhere, you may be sure of one thing—that I do it for pay."

Harriet's writing style was conversation on paper. She didn't have time to polish her phrases, so she just talked in ink. And people loved it.

So did Calvin. He was grateful for the checks received from the Eastern magazine editors, and he was thankful that his wife had an opportunity to develop her talents. Once when she was in New York talking to editors, he wrote her, "My dear, you must be a literary woman. It is so written in the book of fate. Get a good stock of health and brush up your mind. Write yourself fully and always Harriet Beecher Stowe, which is a name euphonious, flowing and full of meaning. Then, your husband will lift up his head in the gate and your children will rise up and call you blessed." The last sentence is quoted from Solomon's reference to an ideal wife in Proverbs 31.

There was good reason for him to be concerned about her health. The birth of her fifth child in four years had left Harriet weak emotionally and physically. At times she felt she was going blind. At other times her headaches were insufferable.

Financial problems worsened and left her in dark moods. "Our straits for money this year," she wrote a friend, "are unparallelled, even in our annals."

Calvin's income had been sliced in half because of the seminary's plight. During these days she wrote, "I suffer with sensible distress of the brain, as I have done more of less since my illness last winter, a distress which some days takes from me all power of planning or executing anything. . . . When one cannot think or remember anything, then what can be done."

Then when her brother George, only one year older, was found shot to death outside his home in Rochester, New York, everything caved in. Emotionally depressed, she stopped writing entirely. About the only thing she could laugh about was the way her husband tried to take charge: "My husband has developed wonderfully as a housefather and nurse. You would laugh to see him in his spectacles, gravely marching the little troop in their nightgowns up to bed, tagging after them, as he says, like an old hen after a flock of ducks."

When her health failed to improve, she eventually went to a sanitorium in Vermont to see if a special water treatment would help.

Those days were more difficult for Calvin than they were for her. Their letters frequently disclosed their love for each other. He loved her, he said, "as much as I am capable of loving a fellow creature."

But the letters also showed Calvin's self-doubts. He wondered if he should give up the ministry, not because of the seminary's dire financial situation but because of his own lack of spirituality. "I try to be spiritually minded," he wrote her, "and I find in myself a most exquisite relish and deadly longing for all kinds of sensual gratification."

She replied devotionally, "My love, you must know the wonderful knowledge of Jesus which so subdues and transforms. You seek knowledge with a burning thirst. Even so you must seek Christ, that you may know him. . . . If you had studied Christ with half the energy that you have studied Luther—if you were as eager for daily intercourse with him as to devour the daily newspaper—then would he be formed in you, the hope of glory. . . . You do not sufficiently control your own mind on this subject—all your carefulness, prudence, caution and honesty I admire and commend—but when you become nervous, anxious, fretful and apprehensive of poverty, then you have taken matters out of Christ's hand into your own."

But the admonition wasn't one-sided. When her letters got gloomy, he wrote back: "Is the high state of spirituality which you seemed to enjoy all gone? It was my chief hope—the darkness and despondency of my own mind—that you could be continually a guide and support to my feeble and tottering steps in the way of life."

When her letters sounded as if she was in "a

high state of spirituality," he took "great comfort amid the terrible sorrow" of his life that his wife was "growing in grace."

In 1850, Calvin and Harriet finally left Cincinnati when he received an opportunity to teach at his alma mater, Bowdoin College, in Maine. During the long winter, Harriet once again had time to write.

But what should she write about? Her sister Catherine urged her to write a story about slavery: "Hattie, if I could use a pen as you can, I would write something that will make this whole nation feel what an accursed thing slavery is."

She asked her brother, Henry Ward Beecher, and he replied, "Do it, Hattie, do it. Write something and I myself will scatter it thick as the leaves of Vallombrosa."

Hattie didn't feel inspired, but she scribbled a few pages on the subject. Calvin picked it up, read the pages slowly, and then responded in tears: "Hattie, this is it. Begin at the beginning, work up to this and you'll have your book."

So she plunged in and soon *Uncle Tom's Cabin* was written. Her first subtitle was "The Man Who Was a Thing," but later she changed it to "Life Among the Lowly."

It appeared first in serial form in the magazine *The National Era*, and Hattie could barely meet the magazine's deadlines. To get out of the house, she used her husband's office at Bowdoin where she could write in tranquillity.

Though the story was an instant success in the magazine, the book publisher wasn't sure he wanted to take a risk on it. He asked Calvin Stowe to put up half the money for the cost of publishing it, but Calvin had no money.

Eventually, he agreed to give the Stowes a 10 percent royalty and printed 5,000 copies. In two days the first edition sold out. The publisher went back to press and three months later had sold out the next edition of 20,000 copies. Then he went back to press again.

Overnight Harriet became a celebrity. The publisher hadn't paid her the first royalty check yet, but he said she could expect a check in the thousands. For several years Calvin's annual salary had only been a thousand dollars.

She traveled to New York City where she was greeted as a star. She wrote back to her husband: "It is not fame nor praise that contents me. I seem never to have needed love so much as now. I long to hear you say that you love me."

When someone suggested that this sudden fame might lead her to pride and vanity, she replied, "You do not have to be afraid of that. You see, I did not write the book."

"What do you mean?" she was asked.

"I was only the instrument. The Lord wrote the book."

Soon *Uncle Tom's Cabin* was printed in England, France, Germany, Italy, and Portugal, and her fame became international. Within a year, she and Calvin had been invited to visit England, all expenses paid.

To a British writer she identified herself with her usual sense of humor, as "a little bit of a woman, somewhat more than forty, about as thin and dry as a pinch of snuff, never very much to look at in my best days and looking like a used up article now."

And her husband? Harriet described him this way: "a man rich in Greek and Hebrew, Latin and Arabic, and also, rich in nothing else."

The tour of England was more fun for Harriet than it was for Calvin. He reported to friends in the States: "Wife bears it all very well. She is meek, humble, pious and loving, the same that she ever was. As for me, I am tired to death of the life I lead here. From the lowest peasant to the highest noble, wife is constantly beset, and I for her sake, so that we have not a moment's quiet."

Everyone from Charles Dickens to the Archbishop of Canterbury seemed enraptured at the thought of shaking hands with Harriet Beecher Stowe. Calvin could hardly believe it.

At one point, he confessed that he was feeling "inexpressibly blue." It wasn't that he was jealous of his wife's fame; it was that he felt that the British were celebrating his wife's book primarily because it criticized something going on in America—slavery. Often, he noticed, when Harriet was introduced, there was a long diatribe against the United States for allowing the sin of slavery to continue.

So this rumpled, roly-poly scholar with heavy side-whiskers picked his occasion to tell off the British. Some 4,000 had gathered in Exeter Hall to commemorate Anti-Slavery Day. It was all very well, he preached at them, for the British to free its slaves, but England itself was fostering slavery by trading with the southern states in the U.S. If England would insist on free-grown cotton—and four-fifths of the American cotton crop was sold to England—slavery would cease in America because of the economic pressure. "Are you willing to sacrifice one penny of your profits to do away with slavery?"

Harriet was proud of her husband, but the crowd booed. And the next day his speech was castigated as an insult to the nation and an outrage against Christianity.

Back in America, Harriet found herself thrust into the role of leader in the anti-slavery movement. What riled her upon her return was that northern clergymen were not unanimous in their condemnation of slavery. So with the help of her brother Edward and her husband, Calvin, she drafted an anti-slavery petition, got 3,000 ministers to sign it, and traveled to Washington, D.C., to present it to Congress.

After Lincoln was elected president and the Civil War had begun, Harriet felt that the end of slavery was at hand. But then she had her doubts. Lincoln had written a letter to Horace Greeley of the *New York Tribune,* which stated, "My paramount object in this struggle is to save the Union and is not to save or destroy slavery. If I could save the Union without freeing any slave, I would do it."

Harriet was horrified. She countered with a letter to the editor, expressing what she imagined Jesus Christ's response would be if He were in Lincoln's place: "My paramount object in this struggle is to set at liberty them that are bruised and not either to save or destroy the Union. What I do in favor of the Union, I do because it helps free the oppressed."

Two years later, Harriet was Lincoln's guest in the White House. The President put out his great hand and took Harriet's small hand in his. "So this is the little lady who made this big war?" he said.

On January 1 she was sitting quietly in the balcony of the Boston Music Hall, enjoying a concert, when a telegram came from Washington, announcing that Abraham Lincoln had signed the Emancipation Proclamation. Cheers erupted throughout the large auditorium, hats were thrown into the air, and people hugged and kissed each other. Then someone spotted Harriet in the balcony and shouted, "Mrs. Stowe! Mrs. Stowe!" Soon the entire Music Hall was ringing with shouts, "Mrs. Stowe! Mrs. Stowe!" She was the little lady who had done the most to rouse the North to the plight of the slave. Perhaps as much as Lincoln himself, she had caused that Proclamation to be written.

But life at home with Calvin was quite mundane compared to the plaudits of the crowds.

Occasionally he chronicled her shortcomings for her. She wasn't the easiest person to live with, he told her: "I am naturally very methodical. Anything out of place is excessively annoying. This is a feeling to which you are a stranger. You have no idea of either time or place. Permanency is my delight; yours everlasting change."

That wasn't all. He continued his criticism: "I am naturally particular, you are naturally slack— and you often give me inexpressible torment without knowing it. You have vexed me beyond endurance often by taking up my newspapers and then instead of folding them properly and putting them in their place, either dropping them all sprawling on the floor, or wabbling them all up into one wabble, and then sprawling them on the table like an old hen with her guts and gizzard squashed out."

His next complaint was: "I am naturally very irritable, take offense easily, utter my vexation in a moment, and then it is gone; you are naturally more forebearing, take offense less easily and are silent and retain the wound."

All of these criticisms of Harriet were contained in a letter Calvin wrote to her while she was traveling. But five days later, he had second thoughts. He apologized for spelling out their differences so sharply, before tacking on a few fresh complaints: "You seldom hesitate to make a promise, whether you have ability to perform it or not, like your father and Kate—only not quite as bad—and promises so easily made are very easily broken."

Harriet's response was a mixture of an apology and a defense. Her main complaint against him was: "If when you have said things hastily and unjustly you would only be willing to retract them in calmer moments. This is what you almost never do. You leave the poisoned arrow in the wound."

But then in a calmer mood she wrote, "With such a foundation for mutual respect and affection as there is in us—with such true and real and deep love, it is good that we can exercise a correcting power over each other—that I might help you to be kind and considerate, and you me to be systematic and regular."

Throughout life, Calvin tended to be the pessimist; she the optimist. He was the pennypincher, who felt every luxury would be a step toward the poorhouse; she, the visionary who always had a fresh dream to replace an old one that had gone sour.

In 1863 Calvin, now sixty, retired from teaching, and Harriet, eight years younger, was planning a dream home for them to live in. Calvin, of course, was not much help, either in dreaming or in building. He was sure that he would be able to say, "I told you so," this time.

But she wrote cheerily: "My house with eight gables is growing wonderfully. I go every day to see it. I am busy with drains, sewers, sinks, digging, trenching and above all with manure. You should see the joy with which I gaze on manure-heaps, in which the eye of faith sees Delaware grapes and d'Angouleme pears, and all sorts of roses and posies."

After they had moved in, Harriet had to admit, albeit reluctantly, that Calvin was probably right this time. Once, Calvin was taking an afternoon snooze in his bedroom when the plumbing in the ceiling erupted and he was ingloriously drenched. One biographer lists the problems: "Pipes were forever bursting, windows jamming, cellars flooding, and other wholly undreamed-of difficulties were always arising. When bills for repairs were added to the high cost of simply maintaining the house, the lawn and the greenhouse, the result was staggering."

Calvin talked about the poorhouse more than ever.

It was about that time that Harriet is said to have prayed, "Lord, don't take me until my dear husband is gone, for nobody else can do for him what I can."

One thing she did for him was to get a manuscript of his published. For years he had been working on a manuscript, a theological work on the origin of the books of the Bible. Though he was one of the foremost theologians of the day, he had a psychological block about putting his thoughts in print. With little success, Harriet had been urging him to complete the manuscript. Finally, she privately contacted a publisher: "In regard to Mr. Stowe, you must not scare him off by grimly declaring that you must have the whole manuscript complete before you set the printer to work. You must take the three quarters he brings you and at least make believe begin printing; and he will immediately go to work and finish the whole; otherwise, what with lectures and the original sin of laziness, it will all be indefinitely postponed. I want you to make a crisis, that he shall feel that now is the accepted time, and that this must be finished first and foremost."

Harriet's plan succeeded. And much to the surprise of the publisher and Calvin, but not to Calvin's optimistic wife, so did the book. It sold extremely well and stopped Calvin's thinking about the poorhouse for awhile.

The Stowes had seven children: the twins, Eliza and Harriet, neither of whom ever married; Henry Ellis; Frederick William; Georgiana May; Samuel Charles, who died of cholera in infancy; and Charles Edward, born when his mother was thirty-nine.

Henry drowned in the Connecticut River near the campus of Dartmouth College where he had been studying. Both Calvin and Harriet were crushed by the tragedy, but it was Harriet who bounced back more quickly. Several times a day for weeks, Calvin visited his son's grave. "I am submissive, but not reconciled," he said. Finally Harriet, pretending that she needed a vacation, coaxed him to take the family to Maine for a few weeks.

But their problem child was Fred, who returned from the Civil War as a captain wounded in military action at Gettysburg. More of a trial was the fact that Fred had become an alcoholic.

For a long time Harriet the optimist refused to admit that her son had a serious problem. Calvin knew better. She buried herself in writing prodigiously and in other projects such as building her new house, so she wouldn't have to think about Fred so much. Between 1863 and 1870 she wrote ten books, a volume of short stories, another of religious poetry, as well as dozens of magazine articles.

Finally, however, unable to ignore Fred's alcoholism any longer, she thought of a way to keep him busy.

What a grandiose scheme it was. She rented an old cotton plantation near Jacksonville, Florida, and installed Fred as manager (even though his knowledge of growing and marketing cotton was nil). She was sure that outdoor work would be good for him. One hundred former slaves would be employed on the project.

Fred's problems with alcohol continued. After two years of failure—both in the cotton business and with staying sober, Fred was switched by his mother to a 200-acre orange grove nearby. Once again the results were disastrous.

A few years later, Fred Stowe disappeared. He was last seen in San Francisco, then was heard of no more.

The loss of this son in whom she had invested so much made an old woman out of Hattie. In a short time her hair turned white.

For several more years she continued writing and even did some lecturing, but when Calvin died in 1886, Harriet's public life stopped. She lived ten more years and then was buried at his side in Andover, Massachusetts.

It was an unusual marriage, especially for the nineteenth century. Though Calvin's fame as a scholar was far eclipsed by his wife's achievements as a popular writer, he seemed sincerely happy with his wife's prestige. In a book she once wrote about Bible characters, her description of Abraham and Sarah may give a clue to her own relationship with Calvin: "While Sarah called Abraham 'lord,' it is quite apparent from certain little dramatic incidents that she expected him to use his authority in the line of her wishes."

In pursuing their separate careers, Calvin and Harriet spent considerable time away from each other. Though they frequently criticized each other, their deep love for one another was obvious.

It was Calvin who had encouraged her to launch her writing career, and it was Calvin who had served as her literary agent both in America and in England in the early stages of her writing.

Calvin had streaks of instability, stemming, no doubt, from his background. During these periods Harriet's strength undergirded the family. When he became moody and pessimistic, she maneuvered him out of his despair. When he was King Saul in a fit of depression, she had to be his King David playing a harp to bring him out of his moods.

A sensitive man who felt he had psychic powers, he was lured by spiritualism after the drowning of their son Henry. Though initially Harriet was toying with the possibility of spirit contact as well—it was the "rage" in those days—she soon realized how unbiblical it was, and tried to dissuade her husband from dabbling with it.

Like many modern marriages, the union of Calvin and Harriet Beecher Stowe was a relationship that can't be put in a box. Each strengthened the other, and probably neither would have achieved fame without the other's support.

CHAPTER
FIVE

Meet
Billy
and
Ruth
Graham

We all know Billy Graham. Or do we?

So much has been written about this internationally famous evangelist that he is recognized immediately wherever he travels around the world.

But what is Billy Graham like when he's at home?

And Ruth Graham? What adjustments has she had to make in her marriage to a man who has become an international celebrity?

By this time in your reading of this book, you know that there are no typical marriages. You can be sure that the Graham marriage isn't typical either. From it you can learn some lessons that will strengthen your own marriage relationship.

She was raised in a missionary compound in China, the daughter of a Presbyterian physician. At night she and her family read the classics and played games together.

He was raised on a dairy farm in North Carolina. His parents didn't talk much about religion. He was more interested in batting averages than in school, and probably thought Dostoevski was a rookie shortstop for the Cincinnati Reds.

In her family, women were outspoken; in his family, the men did the talking.

As a teenager she dreamed of becoming a missionary to an isolated outpost in Tibet. He wanted to be a major league first baseman, with a cud of chewing tobacco in his cheek.

The girl: Ruth McCue Bell. The boy: Billy Frank Graham.

Billy and Ruth Graham have become legendary figures around the world. For three decades he has been among the most admired men in America. One secular magazine called Dr. Graham the best-known man in the world. He has preached to more than one hundred million people in person and many times that number by radio and television. He has visited presidents, prime ministers, and royalty, to say nothing of corporate executives and financial tycoons. Every book he writes is a guaranteed best-seller. Probably more than two million people have made decisions for Christ as a direct result of his ministry.

That's Billy Graham.

Yet as one close observer remarked, "Half Billy is Ruth."

To which she says, "Nonsense."

She also says, "Nonsense," when Billy says, "Heaven is like being married to Ruth."

Billy sometimes veers toward the pious and pontifical; Ruth opts for the practical.

Once when Billy preached a sermon on the Christian home, he asked his wife (as he usually does) what she thought of it.

She responded: "It was a good sermon except for one thing."

"What was that?"

"The timing."

"The what?"

"The timing. You spent eleven minutes on a wife's duty to her husband and only seven on a husband's duty to his wife."

That's the way Ruth is.

She has a mind of her own. Despite Billy's Baptist beliefs, she has remained a staunch Presbyterian.

"At the beginning of our marriage," Ruth recalls, "some very wise person told me that when two people agree on everything, one of them is unnecessary."

Billy and Ruth Graham do not agree on everything. She admits, "Life in the Billy Graham household is not a matter of uninterrupted sweetness and light."

With her evangelistic husband away from home for months at a time, Ruth Graham has had to make some adjustments, but she says, "Although we don't have the usual family life, we have an interesting and fulfilled one."

One of the key reasons for this happiness is a favorite saying of Ruth's: "A happy marriage is a union of two forgivers." Another key reason is the sense of humor that both Billy and Ruth have. "If you don't take things too seriously," Ruth says, "disagreeing can even be a lot of fun."

Billy and Ruth are not at all alike. Billy may have been raised on a farm, and Ruth in a secluded Chinese compound, but she is a far better handyman than he is. A respect for the other's strengths, rather than a harping on the other's weaknesses, has made their marriage grow stronger through the years. In the first few years of marriage there was a lot of give and take, however.

They met as students at Wheaton College (Illinois) in 1940. She was a twenty-year-old sophomore; he was a freshman, but nearly two years older.

He had already come a long way from those days on the farm in North Carolina. In high school he liked to race cars and enjoyed the girls. He loved the excitement of the former and was actually somewhat shy with the latter. But at the age of sixteen, Billy saw an evangelist's finger pointed at him. "I remember a great sense of burden that I was a sinner before God and had a great fear of hell and judgment." Before long, he had walked the aisle and had committed his life to Jesus Christ.

During the rest of his high school days he was, according to his coach, "an interesting, challenging, and inspiring mixture of saint and devil, with a predominant measure of saint."

After graduation, he enrolled in fundamentalist Bob Jones College. He lasted one semester. On the farm he had been footloose; the college's rigid schedule cooped him up. He couldn't stand the confinement. Besides that, school authorities had already scolded him a couple times for stepping over their boundaries.

So he enrolled in another unaccredited school, Florida Bible Institute. It was here that he began preaching. It was also here that he began going steady. By the end of his first year in Florida he was practically engaged. Four months later, however, his girl friend announced to him that she was breaking their "understanding" because she wanted to marry another student. He was crushed.

He wrote to a friend: "All the stars have fallen out of my sky. There is nothing to live for. We have broken up."

Shortly afterward, he made two decisions: one, to be more cautious about his involvement with girls in the future; and two, to zero in on one particular vocation. He wrote home: "Dear Mother and Dad: I feel that God has called me to be a preacher."

Then nearly twenty-two, he headed north to Wheaton College to prepare himself for the ministry. It was his third college, but he was still classified a freshman.

To Billy, whose North Carolina accent could hardly be understood by Midwesterners and who found the raw northern temperatures almost unbearable, Illinois seemed to be a foreign country. In fact, he considered dropping out. But before he could consider it seriously, he met a hazel-eyed brunette from China.

Although Ruth thought him somewhat of a "beanpole," it apparently was love after the first date for her. Just the way he raced up the stairs made her think that he knew where he was going and was in a hurry to get there. She admired that.

Billy was smitten, too, despite his resolution to take it slow with girls. After their first date, he wrote home to his mother that he "just could not believe anyone could be so beautiful and so sweet." Meanwhile Ruth went to her room and "told the Lord that if I could spend the rest of my life serving Him with Bill, I would consider it the greatest privilege imaginable."

Ruth McCue Bell had already lived an eventful twenty-one years. Her father and mother had been married in Waynesboro, Virginia (only a couple of hundred miles from Billy Graham's home near Charlotte), but Dr. Nelson Bell had taken his wife to North China to serve God in a missionary hospital in 1916. It was there, four years later, that Ruth was born, the second of the three Bell daughters.

Those were turbulent days in China. Ruth reminisces: "I can never recall going to sleep at night without hearing gunshots in the countryside around the house." The children were never permitted to leave the mission compound without an adult. In that part of China, warlords, bandits, and kidnappers were all commonplace.

Despite the excitement, Ruth wasn't fearful. "I think the greatest tribute to mother's courage is that we children never sensed fear [in her] and so we ourselves never had any fear."

It was a missionary home full of good humor, books of all kinds—from detective stories to the classics—and enjoyable Bible study. The idea that Bible study should be enjoyable has been a slogan for Ruth.

Her sense of humor probably came from her father: "He could make a joke out of any situation," she says.

Ruth can't recall when she didn't love the

Lord. "My earliest recollections are of deepest gratitude to God for having loved me so much that He was willing to send His Son to die in my place."

Despite their wholesome upbringing, Ruth and her older sister, Rosa, scrapped constantly. "We fought verbally and with our hands and feet, and the servants used to gather around, when our parents were at their afternoon clinic, and try to guess who was going to win."

In the evenings they read the classics (Dickens and Scott were Ruth's favorites) and played word games, Carroms, or Flinch. Bible games on Sunday sharpened their grasp of Scripture facts.

Ruth's mother was concerned about her children's appearance. She didn't want them to look as if their clothes came from a missionary barrel. In agreement with her mother's philosophy, Ruth says, "Not caring about one's appearance goes against a woman's nature."

As Ruth approached teenage years, her mother wrote, "Ruth is growing fast and is somewhat scatterbrained." Maybe she was scatterbrained, but she was also dedicated. She told her sister that she wanted to be "captured by bandits and beheaded, killed for Jesus' sake." When she dared to pray like that, her sister Rosa refused to say "amen." Instead, Rosa countered by praying, "Lord, don't listen to her."

When she heard and read about the needs of Tibet, Ruth became interested in that exotic land, and decided that she was "called" to be an old-maid missionary to Tibet.

For junior high school, Ruth and Rosa, together with three other children, were taught by a tutor, Miss Lucy Fletcher, at their parents' expense. For senior high school she was sent to a mission school in Korea where she "excelled in Bible but not much else." Leaving her parents and going away to school was not easy for her to do. It was not easy on her parents, either. Her father said, "It is certainly the one hard thing that missionaries have to do—have their children so far away during these important years."

But at age seventeen, Ruth was on her way to America and to Wheaton College where she would major in Bible and minor in art. Bible has always been a strong subject for Ruth. Her husband still considers her to be a better Bible student than he is.

Ruth didn't consider Wheaton College as spiritual a school as she needed, and wanted to transfer to Prairie Bible Institute in Canada. Her father's blunt response was, "As long as I pay the bills, you go where I send you."

She stayed. Actually, after she met Bill (she never called him Billy), she was troubled because he seemed to be so serious. She liked the fact that "he knows where he is going," but he didn't seem to have fun doing it. "Every date we had was to a preaching service of some kind. He didn't have enough time to go to ball games." The first time she heard him preach, she wasn't impressed. His wild gestures embarrassed her, and he preached so loudly. *How can I ever sit through all this?* she asked herself.

Ruth had some other misgivings, too. Bill was surprisingly formal when they were together. Having recently been jilted by the girl in Florida, Billy guarded his emotions. Ruth interpreted this as coolness or even disinterest. Yet she knew that he had practically been engaged to one girl and had dated several others. She wondered if he could manage to maintain a relationship longer than a month or two. Opening her Bible at random to Proverbs, she discovered a Scripture verse which reinforced her misgivings. The verse said, "Meddle not with them that are given to change."

But Ruth kept meddling with him anyway. The biggest snag in the relationship was her commitment to return to Tibet as a missionary. She confided in her sister Rosa, who was also a student at Wheaton. Rosa advised her frankly: "You think the Lord is leading you to Tibet, but maybe He might have led you here to meet Billy."

Ruth still wasn't convinced. Even after she and Billy were engaged in the summer of 1941, she had second thoughts. She tried to persuade Bill to go to Tibet with her. He promised to pray about it, but he returned, telling her that he "just had no leading whatsoever" about going to Tibet.

Finally, Billy put it this way: "If you believe that God has brought us together and if you believe that the husband is the head of the wife, then if the Lord is leading me, it's up to you to follow."

About the time that Ruth was finally convinced, Billy had some problems of his own. Ruth's father was a missionary with the Southern Presbyterian Church, a denomination Billy regarded as liberal. How could Dr. Bell be in the will of God and stay in such a denomination? Ruth was incensed that Billy doubted her father's spiritual consecration. Once again the engagement seemed tenuous. (Years later, Billy acknowledged that Ruth and her father were the greatest influences in making his ministry more church-centered.)

Ruth continued to have her doubts, but finally agreed to his proposal of marriage. Billy recalls, "She said she still wasn't sure that she loved me, but she felt led of the Lord that it was God's will for her life." Billy and Ruth were married at Montreat, the Presbyterian conference center in the mountains of North Carolina, in August 1943, two months after his graduation from college.

Biographer John Pollock aptly summarizes Ruth's contribution to Billy this way: "Ruth more than anyone broadened Billy's mind. She had no need to polish his manners or graces, as D. L. Moody's were polished by his wife, but she was cultured, traveled, with a love of art and literature. She saved his seriousness from degenerating into stuffy solemnity, and preserved from extinction the light touch, the slice of small boy. Moreover, Ruth and her family, loyal Presbyterians, eased Billy Graham from his outspoken conviction that a vigorous Scriptural faith could not dwell within the great denominations."

Another biographer, Stanley High, says, "It is her commonsense and household-fashioned wit that help him, when in the clouds, not to get lost there; her unawed attitude is a safeguard, for him, against idiosyncracies, pontifications, and most of all the sin of pride."

The adjustment to married life was not easy for either of them. Years later Billy admitted in an article in *McCall's* magazine, "We did have a difficult time adjusting to this new life and to each other."

Part of Ruth's problem was the transition from a campus life with literature, art, and Bible courses that she loved to the life of a homemaker with household chores. She made no claim to being a skilled cook, except perhaps of Chinese dishes "cooked with plenty of garlic, and Billy didn't care for garlic."

Then there was dishwashing. "I don't like dishwashing. There's no future in it, nothing creative," Ruth says. In high school someone had given her a small plaque which read, "Praise and Pray and Peg Away." She hung it over the sink, where it still is today, but it didn't seem to do much good. "I even made my dissatisfaction with the dishes a definite prayer concern," she says, "and still I couldn't dig up much enthusiasm."

Of course, there were other adjustment problems. She didn't see why Billy always left his desk so cluttered or why he couldn't break the habit of throwing used towels over the top of the bathroom door.

But those were the little irritations that vex every marriage. Billy acknowledges, "We had come from different backgrounds, and suddenly we were on our own. It was hard, and not just because of our different temperaments."

Ruth recalls those early days of marriage and says, "Happy marriages are never accidental. They are the result of good hard work."

And at times they did have to work hard at it.

After their honeymoon, they returned to Western Springs (Illinois) where Billy had just accepted the call to become the pastor of the local Baptist church. That was a problem for two reasons: first, Ruth had never been consulted on the decision, and second, Ruth was a Presbyterian.

Ruth was annoyed that Billy would make such a decision unilaterally. She felt that if they were going to spend the rest of their lives together, any important decision should be discussed and prayed about together.

At first, it wasn't easy for Billy to counsel with Ruth on decisions, but as he grew to appreciate her wisdom, he did it naturally. After the first five years of married life, Billy made few significant decisions without getting Ruth's insight on them. She was the one who suggested the name for his radio broadcast, "The Hour of Decision." She was the one who urged him to go full time into an evangelistic ministry. She was the one who did the major research for his first best-seller, *Peace with God*. And when the Billy Graham Evangelistic Association was formed, Billy wanted Ruth to be on the five-member board of directors with him (and she consented).

However, the bigger problem in Western Springs was that the new pastor at the Baptist church had a wife who was a Presbyterian and refused to become a Baptist. It wasn't that she didn't consider it. She studied the Scriptures, but they didn't convince her that she needed to be rebaptized by immersion.

The situation was helped when the church leaders changed the name of the church to the Village Church, feeling it would have a wider appeal. Among other advantages, the change relieved Ruth of having to change denominations.

During the early days of their marriage, Billy was introduced to a widening circle of friends. Youth for Christ was just beginning and Billy felt privileged to be on the inside of this exciting evangelistic movement. A new radio program called "Songs in the Night," featuring a bass-baritone soloist named George Beverly Shea, was now being broadcast from Billy's church. Ruth helped write the weekly scripts.

Always full of ideas, Billy loved to discuss them with other ministers. While he was discussing and discoursing, Ruth was left alone in their upstairs apartment in Western Springs. It was another problem in their young marriage. Ruth didn't enjoy being taken for granted, and she told him so.

She frequently helped Billy keep things in perspective. He enjoys telling the story of how, early in their marriage, he dropped what he thought was a dollar bill in the collection plate. It was actually a ten-dollar bill, and at that stage in their lives it was a mistake they could hardly afford. He bemoaned his financial loss to Ruth.

"In the Lord's sight," Ruth reminded him, "you'll get credit for only an offering of one dollar—not ten—because that's all you meant to give."

Billy tells the story to help his listeners understand a little about giving, but it also helps one understand a little about Ruth.

As Youth for Christ rallies spread across the country, so did Billy Graham's ministry. Traveling had always fascinated him, and the opportunity to win souls for Christ could not be refused. But it meant being away from home three-fourths of the time.

For Ruth, living in an apartment in a Chicago

suburb far away from family and being separated from her husband of less than two years were not easy adjustments.

She recognized that God had given her husband the gift of evangelism, and that in itself would necessitate their being apart for long periods of time. She also recognized that Billy had a hard time saying no to any invitation to speak. And she couldn't do much about that just then, either.

Not being able to change his situation, she decided to change her own. She "simply packed her bags," and moved down to North Carolina where her parents, now home from China, were living. "I realized that it was going to be like this from now on," she explains, "and that he was going to be gone most of the time. In a case like ours, I believe the family is the Lord's business, but a husband should have his wife settled where she's going to be happy."

Living near her parents made it easier on Ruth, but for the girl who had aspired to a lifetime in isolated Tibet, loneliness seemed part of the divine game plan.

Billy says, "My wife and I have both had to be dedicated on this point—and Ruth has great gifts for it."

She keeps a stiff upper lip and tries not to acknowledge pain of any kind—emotional or physical. She says of the frequent separations from Billy: "You get used to it. You keep busy.

The best thing for any of us is keeping busy."

Speaking of her earlier desire to be a missionary to Tibet, Ruth wrote in *The Ladies Home Journal:* "I think that the Lord must have given me that intense longing for a purpose, so that I could have the understanding and the sense of fulfillment that I receive now from Bill's work. I knew from the very beginning that I wouldn't be in first place in his life. Christ would be first. Knowing that, accepting that, solves an awful lot of problems right there. So I can watch him go with no regrets, and wait for him joyfully."

But when they have been together, Billy and Ruth have shared much and have contributed much to each other's lives.

Their children (Virginia, born 1945; Anne, born 1948; Ruth (nicknamed "Bunny"), born 1950; William Franklin, born 1952; and Nelson Edman, born 1958) made it difficult for Ruth to travel frequently with her husband even when his ministry had grown to such proportions that traveling was affordable.

Grandparents helped in the raising of the children, but Ruth, of course, missed having Billy around for many reasons. Much of the disciplining was left to her ("I played them like a xylophone," she says). And the young children did not provide the mental stimulation that Ruth's active mind craved. "There's nothing greatly stimulating about wiping noses or cleaning muddy shoes and the dirt they leave. A mother just must realize that God put her there."

As a homemaker in Montreat, North Carolina, she handled the family finances, did the carpentry (although she insists that her husband could hit a nail with a hammer if he put his mind to it), and even supervised the building of their new home when the first one became too much of a tourist attraction.

In the home, Ruth still keeps a Bible open on a special desk. "When Bill is away, I'm likely to have the Book open to Proverbs. It's got more practical help in it than ten books on child psychology."

Here are some principles of her home drawn from Proverbs: "Put happiness in the home before neatness. . . . In discipline be firm but patient. . . . Teach that right means behaving as well as believing."

Frequently Billy's letters stated, "If you were only here, I could talk over my sermon with you." He always knew he could get an honest evaluation from Ruth; he missed her perceptive insight.

On long crusades, Ruth tried to be with him at least one week of the meetings. But she never wanted to leave her children for long periods. "A mother, like the Lord, needs to be a very present help in time of trouble."

One time that Ruth did accompany Billy, however, was to Great Britain in 1954. It was Billy's second trip there and he had toned down his Youth for Christ wardrobe, which had been characterized by bright socks and ties. Remembering what he had learned from his prior experience in England, he suggested to Ruth that she might not want to wear lipstick because most church people in London did not.

Ruth didn't readily accept the suggestion: "Don't you think that that may be something on which the Lord expects us to help their understanding?"

In her diary Ruth recorded the incident: "Bill stooped from being a man of God to become a meddlesome husband and ordered my lipstick off. There was a lively argument—then I wiped it off. He got so busy getting the bags together I managed to put more on without notice."

Later Ruth explained, "It doesn't seem to me to be a credit to Christ to be drab."

The British Crusades in 1954 and 1955 were monumental. At Wembley, despite almost continual rain, crowds of 50,000 to 80,000 gathered each night to hear the American evangelist.

More unnerving than the huge crowds, however, were the invitations to be guests of royalty. Ruth wrote home, "You should have heard all the titles and seen all the jewels and decorations—and me in a homemade number with zipper trouble."

When they were invited to meet the Queen Mother, Ruth wrote a play-by-play description of the scene to her parents: "Our little tan Ford drove up to the gate at 11:45. . . . We all went to a side room where we talked about golf and the Cockrell-Marciano fight. Then suddenly the door opened: 'Her Majesty the Queen Mother will receive Dr. and Mrs. Graham.' . . . The Queen Mother came toward us with her hand outstretched and I didn't know whether to curtsy first and shake hands later or shake hands first and then curtsy. I don't know which I did. Bill—the merciless wretch—said it looked as though I'd tripped over the rug. . . ."

During the London Crusade, Ruth wrote home, "I am the world's worst soul winner," but night after night she was counseling those who came forward for salvation. One of those to whom she witnessed was British movie star Joan Winmill, who later said, "I didn't know then she was Mrs. Billy Graham. But the first thought that came to my mind when I saw her was how much sooner people like me might have been attracted to Christianity if we had met a few such attractive Christians."

Meanwhile, back in North Carolina, friends had been gathering funds to help the Grahams build a new home. Tourists had been overrunning their yard at the house on Assembly Drive. Sick at home one day, Ruth looked up to see a face pressed against the bedroom window. And when Billy was home, he would sometimes crawl on his hands and knees under his study window to keep from being observed by sightseers passing by on the road above the house.

Ruth immediately went to work on the planning of the new home. According to biographer John Pollock, "She scoured the mountains, buying old timber from disused cabins and brick from an ancient schoolhouse to build a place which fitted exactly into his background. Soon it looked a hundred years old, even to the split-rail fences."

Ever since 1955, this mountainside home has been a haven for Billy. Ruth describes it as "a kind of eagle's nest." Over the years a succession of loyal, faithful helpers have assisted the Grahams around the house and with the children. Each one has been special to the family and has contributed greatly to the children's development. With five children and an assortment of pets, Ruth used to describe it as "a Noah's ark of happy confusion."

But living in a mountain retreat didn't make the times of separation from Billy any shorter or easier for Ruth. In the early years of marriage she sometimes went to bed with his "old, rough sportscoat," because she missed him so much. The fact that she has had few close friends apart from her own parents may have aggravated the situation. Her daughter Bunny says, "I don't know if you can say Mother has a close friend. She doesn't confide in friends that much. Really, the Lord is her best friend."

Ruth has always been somewhat of a free

spirit, and Billy has allowed her to keep her individuality. "She is allowed to be Ruth," says Julie Nixon Eisenhower in her book *Special People*.

As Billy Graham became a national figure, presidents courted his favor, his counsel, and sometimes his influence with voters. In 1960, during the Kennedy-Nixon campaign, *Life* magazine solicited an article from him on why he had decided to vote for Nixon. Ruth had asked him not to write it, wanting him to stay out of politics, and he was hesitant, but after receiving long-distance phone calls from Henry Luce, *Life*'s publisher, Billy consented. He prepared the article and then prayed that the Lord would stop its publication if it were not God's will that it should see print. John F. Kennedy heard of the prospective article and pressured *Life*'s editors to pull it out at the last minute. Ruth was relieved.

She has always cautioned her husband against political involvement. Once in 1964, she and Billy were invited to the White House to be guests of President Lyndon Johnson. At the dinner table LBJ asked Billy who he thought would make a good vice-presidential running mate for him in the forthcoming campaign.

Under the table, Ruth dug her shoes into Billy's shins, her way of reminding him to stay away from politics.

Billy, who always has delighted in teasing his wife, asked her with seeming innocence, "Why did you kick me?"

She wasted no time in answering: "You're supposed to give advice only on spiritual matters."

For the moment, that ended the discussion, but as soon as Lady Bird escorted Ruth out of the room, LBJ asked the evangelist, "Now that they've gone, what do you really think?"

But away from the limelight of the crusades and the dinners with presidents and royalty, Billy and Ruth had concerns about their children. Billy realized that his children were having problems in growing up with an absentee father, and certain things in his personality made it hard to develop a closeness with his children.

Ruth prayed about it, then asked Bill to let her administer discipline in his absence, rather than letting it pile up for him to handle on his return. Otherwise, the children would grow to dread their father's coming home. Subsequently, there has always been mutual love and companionship.

It was their fourth child and eldest son who had special problems in growing up. "He was into everything you can think of," admits Billy. His life style was a concern to the parents, but they tried not to allow it to break their relationship with him. Eventually, the son returned to the Lord and became involved in Christian ministry himself.

But looking back on the darker days, Billy recalls, "During that time, we would hug each other when we met. You need to keep their love at any cost. Because when they come through it, they'll still have that there. When it was over with Franklin, there was no relationship to reestablish; it had been there all along."

The relationship between Billy and Ruth has grown stronger through the years. Daughter Bunny says that she has never heard a harsh word between them.

Ruth explains casually, "During the years, we really haven't had a chance to get tired of each other. So I think we'll just hang in there a little longer."

Teasing and kidding are a part of their sharing, but another part of it consists of serious discussions. Now that the children are grown, Ruth has more time than ever for reading as well as for poetry, painting, and sewing—all of which she enjoys. Over the years she read the writings of Dostoevski and Tolstoi and their biographies because she especially enjoyed these writers. They stretched her mind and gave her a new appreciation of history.

Billy enjoys her input. His sermon illustrations sometimes are derived from books that Ruth has shared with him. "You know how well read Ruth is," he once said; "she seems to know everything about everything"—a remarkable accolade for a husband to give his wife. "Some of my best thoughts come from her," he admits.

Always polite, even to Ruth, Billy has grown in his ability to show his care and interest. "For some reason," Billy's sister says, "the older he's gotten, the freer and more expressive his body language has become." Other family members have noticed it, too. One said, "He used to just shake hands when he'd see me or another member of his family. But now he'll throw those long arms around us and just hug us."

As they have grown older, Billy and Ruth have each shown increasing concern for the other's health. Once when Billy was away on a crusade, Ruth had a small therapeutic pool built at the back of the house. When he returned, he was unhappy with the extravagance. All she said was, "It's cheaper than a funeral" and she walked away.

Both remain active people. In her book *Special People* Julie Nixon Eisenhower asks with some degree of amazement, "How many other grandmothers take up hang-gliding in their fifties?" Ruth did. And the first time she jumped from a steep bank, she hit the ground hard. Later she fell out of a tree when she was putting up a swing for her grandchildren, resulting in injuries so severe that it was a week before she regained consciousness. Julie continued, "And how many grandmothers borrow their son's black leather jacket and go vrooming along mountain roads on a Harley-Davidson? A daring driver, Ruth (and her motorcycle) ended up in a ditch once, in a lake another time."

Ruth smiles about her new-found adventures

and says, "There's no fool like an old fool."

Ruth is no stereotype of an evangelist's wife. Her view of marriage is not a chain of command in which the wife is directly under the husband, but rather a triangle with God at the top, and the husband and wife at the bottom. The husband, she says, "has certain responsibilities and final authority, but marriage is best characterized by mutual submission, not merely the submission of the wife to the husband."

Billy's view is not quite the same. Quoting the verse in Genesis, "He shall rule over thee," Billy says that injunction "has never changed. . . . The wife is to fit into the world of the husband."

In the Graham marriage you see both views from time to time. Ruth has certainly fit into the world of her husband, and she has been content with that. But Ruth's individuality is unflappable, and mutual submission is prominent in the household.

They've come from two different worlds; they live in two different worlds, but together they have built a strong relationship that has brought blessing to the world.

Billy's active life takes him to the masses. Ruth says, "I have an antipathy for platforms." She prefers books, and often keeps four with her: "One book to stimulate me. One book to relax me. One book for information and one book for conversation." And then Ruth says, "And I love nature. I just love to hear the wind in the trees. I love to hear birds. And mostly, I just love to listen to silence."

Ruth was asked to give advice to a young woman about to be married. Said Ruth: "Don't expect your husband to be what only Jesus can be. Don't expect him to give you the security, the joy, the peace, the love that only God Himself can give you."

BIBLIOGRAPHY

THE CALVINS

Bainton, Roland. *Women of the Reformation*. Minneapolis: Augsburg Publishing House, 1971.

Hyma, Albert. *The Life of John Calvin*. Grand Rapids, MI: Wm. B. Eerdmans Publishing Co., 1943.

Johnson, E.M. *Man of Geneva*. Carlisle, PA: The Banner of Truth, 1977.

Martin-Taylor, Duncan. *God's Man*. Grand Rapids, MI: Baker Book House, 1979.

McNeil, John T. *The History and Character of Calvinism*. Fair Lawn, NJ: Oxford University Press, Inc., 1954.

Parker, T.H.L. *Portrait of Calvin*. Philadelphia: Westminster Press, 1954.

Van Halsema, Thea. *This Was John Calvin*. Grand Rapids, MI: Zondervan Publishing House, 1959.

THE CAREYS

Drewery, Mary. *William Carey*. Grand Rapids, MI: Zondervan Publishing House, 1979.

Marshman, John. *Life and Labours of Carey, Marshman, and Ward*. London: Ward Publishers, 1867.

Smith, George. *The Life of William Carey*. London: J.N. Dent and Sons, 1885.

Stevenson, P.M. Grand Rapids, MI: Zondervan Publishing House, 1953.

THE JUDSONS

Anderson, Courtney. *To the Golden Shore*. Grand Rapids, MI: Zondervan Publishing House, 1977.

Hefley, James C. *How Great Christians Met Christ*. Chicago: Moody Press, 1973.

Miller, Basil. *Ann Judson: Heroine of Ava*. Grand Rapids, MI: Zondervan Publishing House, 1947.

THE STOWES

Bradford, Gamaliel, ed. *Portraits of American Women*. New York: Houghton Mifflin Co., 1919.

Gerson, Noel B. *Harriet Beecher Stowe: A Biography*. New York: Praeger Publishing, 1976.

Johnston, Johanna. *Runaway to Heaven*. Garden City, NY: Doubleday & Co., Inc., 1963.

Stowe, Charles Edward. *The Life of Harriet Beecher Stowe*. Boston: Houghton-Mifflin, 1889.

Wilson, Robert F. *Crusader in Crinoline: The Life of Harriet Beecher Stowe*. Philadelphia: J.B. Lippincott Co., n.d.

THE GRAHAMS

Eisenhower, Julie Nixon. *Special People*. New York: Simon & Schuster, Inc., 1979.

High, Stanley. *Billy Graham*. New York: McGraw-Hill Book Co., 1956.

Pollock, John. *Billy Graham*. New York: McGraw-Hill Book Co., 1966.

_____. *A Foreign Devil in China*. Grand Rapids, MI: Zondervan Publishing House, 1971.

CHRISTIAN HERALD ASSOCIATION AND ITS MINISTRIES

CHRISTIAN HERALD ASSOCIATION, founded in 1878, publishes The Christian Herald Magazine, one of the leading interdenominational religious monthlies in America. Through its wide circulation, it brings inspiring articles and the latest news of religious developments to many families. From the magazine's pages came the initiative for CHRISTIAN HERALD CHILDREN'S HOME and THE BOWERY MISSION, two individually supported not-for-profit corporations.

CHRISTIAN HERALD CHILDREN'S HOME, established in 1894, is the name for a unique and dynamic ministry to disadvantaged children, offering hope and opportunities which would not otherwise be available for reasons of poverty and neglect. The goal is to develop each child's potential and to demonstrate Christian compassion and understanding to children in need.

Mont Lawn is a permanent camp located in Bushkill, Pennsylvania. It is the focal point of a ministry which provides a healthful "vacation with a purpose" to children who without it would be confined to the streets of the city. Up to 1000 children between the ages of 7 and 11 come to Mont Lawn each year.

Christian Herald Children's Home maintains year-round contact with children by means of an *In-City Youth Ministry*. Central to its philosophy is the belief that only through sustained relationships and demonstrated concern can individual lives be truly enriched. Special emphasis is on individual guidance, spiritual and family counseling and tutoring. This follow-up ministry to inner-city children culminates for many in financial assistance toward higher education and career counseling.

THE BOWERY MISSION, located at 227 Bowery, New York City, has since 1879 been reaching out to the lost men on the Bowery, offering them what could be their last chance to rebuild their lives. Every man is fed, clothed and ministered to. Countless numbers have entered the 90-day residential rehabilitation program at the Bowery Mission. A concentrated ministry of counseling, medical care, nutrition therapy, Bible study and Gospel services awakens a man to spiritual renewal within himself.

These ministries are supported solely by the voluntary contributions of individuals and by legacies and bequests. Contributions are tax deductible. Checks should be made out either to CHRISTIAN HERALD CHILDREN'S HOME or to THE BOWERY MISSION.

Administrative Office: 40 Overlook Drive, Chappaqua, New York 10514
Telephone: (914) 769-9000